BIZARRE WORLD

A Collection of the World's Creepiest, Strangest, and Sometimes Most Hilarious Traditions

E. REID ROSS

Adams Media
New York   London   Toronto   Sydney   New Delhi

Aadamsmedia

Adams Media
An Imprint of Simon & Schuster, Inc.
57 Littlefield Street
Avon, Massachusetts 02322

First Adams Media hardcover edition August 2019

ADAMS MEDIA and colophon are trademarks of Simon & Schuster.

For information about special discounts for bulk purchases, please contact Simon & Schuster Special Sales at 1-866-506-1949 or business@simonandschuster.com.

The Simon & Schuster Speakers Bureau can bring authors to your live event. For more information or to book an event contact the Simon & Schuster Speakers Bureau at 1-866-248-3049 or visit our website at www.simonspeakers.com.

Interior design by Colleen Cunningham
Interior images © Clipart.com

Manufactured in the United States of America

10 9 8 7 6 5 4 3 2 1

Library of Congress Cataloging-in-Publication Data has been applied for.

ISBN 978-1-5072-1078-9
ISBN 978-1-5072-1079-6 (ebook)

CONTENTS

RITES OF PASSAGE 39

LOVE, MARRIAGE, AND COURTSHIP 73

WORK 103

ENTERTAINMENT 125

FOOD 167

NATURE 195

DEATH 227

INTRODUCTION

Spitting on newborn babies to keep away evil spirits?

Sucking down a glass of bat's blood for health?

Showing up at your neighbor's door with a horse skull and expecting to be let in, no questions asked?

Totally strange, right?

Sure, people take their own customs for granted, but those customs can look pretty bizarre when viewed from a distance. But the truth is, the world is bubbling over with weird customs, rituals, festivals, and overall general weirdness. And in these pages, you'll find plenty of weird to go around, including:

- Camel wrestling in Turkey
- A roadkill-cooking contest in the United States
- Teeth sharpening in the Mentawai Islands
- Turning deceased relatives into jewelry in South Korea
- Stuffing ferrets down your pants in England

Thankfully, some of these customs only happened in the distant past, but some of them are still going on today, even if they're not quite as extreme as they used to be (and some of them are pretty damn extreme!). But if you read about enough of this bizarre stuff, you may get some insight into why in the world anyone participates in these things. Or maybe you'll just sit in slack-jawed wonder, amazed at the things people do (and did) to themselves and others in the name of tradition.

Who knows? Maybe you'll even find a ritual you want to add to your own life! (Though it might be good to avoid the Philippine practice of hanging up coffins containing your dead relatives around town. In most parts of the world people tend to frown on that sort of thing.)

Anyway, let's get started on our bizarre journey. Warning: Great strangeness ahead!

HEALTH AND CHILDBIRTH

11

SPITTING FOR LUCK

Let's Hope That Baby Forgets What You Just Did

GREECE

Okay, sure, in every society on earth, you can safely bet there are customs and superstitions to keep babies healthy and safe from harm. Harmless little rituals that don't do any lasting damage to an infant's self-esteem. Except in the case of Greece. Where they spit right in their fat little faces.

Hawking a loogie directly into a newborn's innocent mug is just one of the ways Greek people incorporate casual spitting in their daily lives. Not that it always involves an actual hunk of phlegm. Some Greeks just make a "ftou" sound. If you hear someone going, "ftou, ftou, ftou," don't worry; they're just warding off the evil eye (with the three spits representing the Holy Trinity). Fishermen have been known to "ftou" onto their nets to help them catch more fish. Not the kind of fish that get regularly invited to fancy dinner parties, we'll assume.

Greeks also believe that when you sneeze it means that someone, somewhere, is thinking about you. If you ask someone for three random numbers, add them together and match the result to the corresponding letter of the alphabet: It will be the first initial of whoever's doing the thinking.

But back to the baby spitting thing. What it's supposed to accomplish is to keep the devil at bay, because we all know that what the ruler of a realm filled with sulfur, brimstone, and everlasting torment hates most is a little saliva. If you have trouble believing that people would do such a thing to an innocent child, just watch *My Big Fat Greek Wedding* again. Look for the scene where the main character, Toula, explains to her husband-to-be that her family is not, in fact, insane but is spewing onto a young member of the brood to keep it free from Satan's clutches.

Surprisingly, Greece isn't the only place where spitting on wee folk is considered normal:

- In Bulgaria, not only do you spit on the kid; after the deed is done you must exclaim, "May the chickens poop on you!" to make the baby seem less appetizing to dark forces.
- The Maasai of Kenya and Tanzania spit at one another in greeting, and newborns get a faceful at birth.
- Infants get the same treatment in Mauritania, as Wolof tribal elders will spit into kids' ears and rub it all over their heads like a slimy salve. This is supposed to

A Sneeze of Great Portent

The Ancient Greeks thought sneezes were signs of prophecy. In 401 B.C.E., the Athenian general Xenophon delivered an inspiring speech to his men, encouraging them to fight despite being completely surrounded by Persians. At the conclusion one of the soldiers let loose with a sneeze. It was considered such a good omen that everyone immediately bowed down.

convey blessings, as saliva is believed to hold the power of words. As their saying goes, "Like honey in water, speech, good or bad, dissolves in saliva which retains part of its power."

The Igbo tribe of Nigeria believes that oration skills can be passed on by an elder chewing some alligator pepper, spitting the results onto a finger, and then sticking that finger into a baby's mouth. Yum!

The origins of the Greek habit of launching saliva projectiles at unsuspecting tots likely have roots in pre-Christian religion. Compared to some of their other customs, it seems downright boring. For instance, in Greek Christmas folklore hideous, deformed goblins called *kallikantzaroi* spend most of the year underground, sawing away at the World Tree in an effort to destroy the earth. But when December 25 rolls around, right before the Tree is about to collapse, they're allowed to venture up to the surface. There, they forget all about their global destruction plans and spend the day playing pranks on humans. Presumably you can keep safe through an adequate amount of spitting. Other early holdovers include a fear of Tuesday (not Friday) the thirteenth and a superstition

Bringing a Knife to a Fistfight

Another way to accidentally find yourself in the middle of an unwanted brawl is to hand someone a knife in Greece. The proper etiquette is to lay it down, then let the other party pick it up. Otherwise it's believed that fisticuffs will surely follow.

about shoes: Leaving them lying around sole-side up after taking them off could lead to a grave case of bad luck. Maybe even death. There's also a belief that when you and someone else say the same thing at the same time, it's a bad omen. When that happens it's believed you'll both have an uncontrollable urge to fight, so to prevent a violent incident the parties must say, "*piase kokkino*," meaning "touch red." The two then must find something red to touch to make everything hunky-dory (possibly wine, which could easily make a fight go away). And, go figure, spitting on one another might even help de-escalate the situation.

Basically, should you ever find yourself in Greece, the key to social success is to just keep spitting nonstop like the world's most belligerent llama—on babies, new acquaintances, strangers, priests, law enforcement, what have you. It's like someone created a heaven for bad-tempered professional baseball managers. So go ahead, be the life of the party. Just be sure to carry something red, watch out for yuletide goblins, and memorize that line about pooping chickens should you accidentally cross the border into Bulgaria.

HEALING BLOOD MILK
Whole, Skim, or Type O Positive?

KENYA Most of us take for granted the fact that we drink milk that doesn't come from our own mothers or even our own species. But when you really think about it—ewww! Gross! Drinking the fluids pulled from the massive teats of a slow-moving cow or goat doesn't sound too appetizing when you dwell on it, right? Well, if that didn't ruin your morning cereal, this might: The Maasai tribe of Kenya (and also Tanzania) love to drink milk just as much as we do, only instead of pasteurizing it they prefer to mix in steaming-hot blood. That's right! Blood!

They get the blood from the same place as the milk, only the process is a little more...stabby. To ensure tasty freshness, they make a small cut in the jugular vein of whichever unlucky cow's turn it is that day. They catch the blood that spills out and mix it in with the milk. Not too much blood, mind, so the wound will heal in a matter of days and the procedure can be repeated. It's like the story of the farmer's three-legged pig: A cow that nice you don't eat all at once.

They use the blood-infused milk in a variety of ways. For instance, as a celebratory drink and as an elixir for the sickly. They keep the mixture in an empty pumpkin and then let the milk ferment with the blood. Bovine urine is sometimes added

No Lion Down on the Job

If it hasn't dawned on you yet, the Maasai are pretty hardcore. For young men to become fully accepted as adult members of the tribe, they used to undergo a ritual called *Moran*. This required that they spend a considerable amount of time alone out in the wild, fending for themselves in the bush. The most intense part of this rite of passage was where they had to kill a lion (when the big cat population was higher) using nothing but a spear. No shield, no extra spear, no Taser...nothing. The ones who survived earned a double–sided beaded leather shoulder strap called an *imporro*, which presumably had "BAD MOTHERF******" embroidered somewhere on it.

in (for that special flavor), and the daytime heat quickly turns it all, according to Exploring-Africa.com, into a kind of "thick, sour and dark-colored yoghurt." For those few who may still be thinking something like "That's no big deal. The British eat blood pudding!" we encourage you to read this paragraph again, as you must have missed the part about the cow pee.

You might think having this as part of their diet would be disastrous for the Maasai people's health. But research has shown their overall fitness is superb, with cholesterol counts being about half of the average American's. Obviously they have a more varied diet than exsanguinated livestock yogurt for breakfast, lunch, and dinner. And their activity levels far exceed any Westerner who isn't an avid triathlete. But the disturbing dish doesn't appear to be a problem. It's also rather revealing that studies have found that Maasai who have moved into cities have markedly higher rates of heart trouble.

Drinking a brew that's filled to the brim with animal fats and protein most likely comes in handy with another custom: the jumping dance. Referred to as *adamu* in the Maasai tongue, this high-energy presentation involves twelve men moving in unison without the aid of drums or any other kind of instrument. This dance begins with women singing, which prompts the men to begin leaping higher and higher to celebrate the coming of age of the young men of the village (seems like the least they could do, as we're talking about the kids who had to go out and fight a lion). The young women get involved as well by dancing and flirting with the young warriors.

It should be pretty clear by now, based on how many times we've mentioned this particular beast in the previous paragraphs, that the cow is a central part of Maasai life. Their seminomadic lifestyle means they follow their herds across the grasslands and use the animals as a form of barter. Cowhides

Not a Good Choice for a Bullfight, Though

Considering their taste in beverages, it shouldn't be surprising that the traditional robe the Maasai wear (called the *shuka*) is blood red. Not only does that color represent courage, strength, and unity; it's also believed to be effective at scaring away lions. The Maasai also tend to wear a lot of bright beaded jewelry in colors that signify various parts of their culture. For instance, blue is for the sky and rain that nourishes them and their cattle. White is pure like the milk from those cattle (until it gets the blood treatment, we suppose). Green is for the land that provides vegetables and grass for their livestock, while yellow represents the life-giving sun. Finally, orange means friendship and generosity, two things that are very important to the Maasai.

provide clothing and shelter, and if you think the Native Americans were good at using every part of an animal, we again encourage you to reread that paragraph that talked about cow pee. As their most prized and valuable possessions, it's said that a good cow is just as important to a Maasai tribesman as an exotic sports car is to a Westerner. That is, if you went out and siphoned out some gasoline to pour over your oatmeal every morning for breakfast.

BABY TOSSING

What Else Are You Going to Do When You Run Out of Horseshoes?

 INDIA

When a brand-new life is brought into the world, just about every culture does unpleasant things to it:

- You get dunked in water.
- A rabbi make a pass over your genitals with a knife.
- You're passed from relative to relative so they can make horrible faces at you, trying to get you to smile or something.

But there aren't that many traditions reserved for motorcycle daredevils and trapeze artists. One such death-defying, high-risk practice still occurs every first week of December in parts of India, where people toss infants off a roof to show their faith in a higher power.

Most popular in the central/southwestern states of Maharashtra and Karnataka, hurling babies from unsafe heights has been going on for around seven hundred years. You'd think more people would know about this.

The site most famous for this ceremony is the Islamic shrine called Baba Umer Dargah, located in the city of Solapur. There's a platform, about fifty feet in the air. That's where the babies are tossed from. They're caught (hopefully) in a sheet held by both Muslims and Hindus. The point isn't to terrify the babies so they learn to shriek at maximum volume—that's just a by-product. The belief is that baby tossing will ensure health and prosperity for the families of little bundles of joy. Hundreds of people show up to watch the spectacle. However, we have to assume health and happiness for the parents might be in jeopardy when the kid grows up and remembers what they did to him.

The practice of baby tossing supposedly originated with an unnamed saint (one who probably had a warped sense of humor) who gave people hope at a time when infant mortality was frighteningly high and medical options were few. His suggestion was that parents build a shrine and lob their offspring from the top. When he somehow got people to agree to this dubious practice, it's said that a sheet appeared miraculously in midair and delivered the airborne youngsters to the ground. In the years that followed, the people's faith that a miracle would save the babies was replaced by non-magical sheets.

The formerly obscure ritual received global attention in 2009 when a film crew captured the phenomenon and

Monthly Seclusion

For the Kalash people of neighboring Pakistan, it's the mothers who have to suffer. Their culture considers the act of childbirth so repugnant and unclean that special buildings (called *Bashleni*) are constructed for women to have their babies in complete seclusion. The men find menstruation equally repulsive, so when that time of the month rolls arounds, it presents another reason for women to be sent to the *Bashleni*.

Lathmar Holi

Women and babies aren't the only ones in India who get the short end of the stick. In the ancient city of Jodhpur, located in the state of Rajasthan, unmarried males get the *entire* stick. During the festival called *Lathmar Holi*, women get the opportunity to whack eligible bachelors with lengthy poles in a recreation ceremony that celebrates the life of Krishna. As the story goes, when the god was young, he and his immature friends had a habit of teasing his beloved, Radha. Finding this behavior quite rude, Radha's friend took up arms in the form of sticks and chased the men away.

broadcast it to a horrified viewing public. Unsurprisingly, people began to call for a ban on the practice. The deputy commissioner for the Bijapur district said, "As I am new to the district, I did not know about the unusual ritual, which is inhuman and terrifying for babies. I intend to prevent the people from indulging in such acts [in future]." The Karnataka State Commission for Protection of Child Rights also got involved, and a hullabaloo ensued. But you know what they found? No record of any child ever being injured in the tossing events. Not one. Public anger soon turned to appreciation, as an editor from the *Lonely Planet* travel guide put it, for India's "rich festival tradition, which allows us to see the country at its most colourful and chaotic." This from someone who never got chucked off a fifty-foot-high platform when *he* was a baby.

As Indian children grow to an age when they have children themselves, they're still not free from distressing rituals. During solar eclipses, pregnant women are encouraged by astrologers to stay indoors, and bathing in holy sources of water is thought to promote health and willpower. And in 2009, during the longest eclipse of the new century, it was discovered that parents had buried thirty-four of their children up to their necks in mud in the belief it would cure them of any disabilities. (It probably cured them of any affection for their parents at any rate.) Unlike baby tossing, the concern over this one didn't fade away. The authorities threatened to prosecute those involved and kicked off an awareness campaign. There are a whole lot of superstitions in India, though (like the fear of getting a haircut on Saturday), so initiatives like this tend to be an uphill battle.

Indeed, superstition in India is considered to be a big social problem. Not only the poor and uneducated but the literate and well-to-do also have unscientific beliefs that vary from region to region. They range from the relatively harmless to the genuinely horrifying. Although traditions like *sati* (the burning or burying alive of widows) and human sacrifice are gradually being relegated to history (because less human sacrifice makes life better, right?), incidents of both still occur. Which makes a little baby hurling every now and again seem a lot less horrifying.

FROG JUICE

You Can Add Wheatgrass, but It Won't Change Much

PERU

Health drinks can be a little hard to swallow sometimes, as anyone who's ever choked down a bottle of kombucha can confirm. No matter how much honey, fruit, or packets of Splenda you toss into the blender, it's hard to cover up the taste of kale to the point where it doesn't taste like the south end of a northbound alpaca. In Peru, however, they've come up with a supposedly rejuvenating concoction that is thoroughly impossible to make taste like anything other than exactly what it is: frog juice.

This is a culinary delicacy in some parts of South America's third-biggest country. *Jugo de rana* (literally a whole frog thrown into a blender along with some herbs and honey) has its origins in ancient mystical folklore. It's also called "Peruvian Viagra," due to its supposed positive effects on erectile dysfunction. So guys, if you're having any, ahem, difficulties, you might want to go frog hunting. But keeping things up isn't the only thing amphibian squeezings can treat:

- Anemia
- Tuberculosis
- Asthma

If you've got any of these conditions, you can benefit from gulping down slimy, mulched pond hoppers. As a bonus, the specific type of critter used as the main ingredient is the Titicaca water frog (*Telmatobius culeus*). If that wasn't hilarious enough, that particular frog's nickname happens to be, because of its baggy, wrinkly appearance, "the scrotum frog."

Frog juice is not some niche drink that's consumed only by a small minority who are immune to nausea; it's very popular. Purveyors of the stuff are murdering so many scrotum frogs, in fact, that they're sliding rapidly toward extinction. To be fair, an increase in pollution is also killing them off in droves, which would seem to argue against their continued ability to produce healthy erections (unless this condition also happens to be a heretofore-unknown side effect of sucking in industrial waste). The Peruvian government is taking measures to save the species by prosecuting illegal wildlife traders and raiding frog juice vendors (who individually go through fifty to seventy containers of the stuff per day). But as the demand remains, your local frog juice dealer will be out there. After all, supernatural

Cuteness on a Stick

While you're sipping your pleasant, cool beverage made from minced frogs, perhaps you'd care for some fried guinea pigs for the main course? That's right, the cute and cuddly rodent that's been a beloved first pet for generations of American children is definitely on the menu in Peru. You can buy them barbecued on a stick by the roadside or order them right off the menu at most restaurants.

medical beliefs of our ancestors supersede bureaucrats telling us that puréeing frogs is wrong.

Conservationists and zoos across the world are making efforts to save the scrotum frog, despite the fact that it looks like something the cat threw up. People like James Garcia, an outreach programs specialist for the Denver Zoo, have been able to look past the frog's flappy repulsiveness and work toward its salvation. He explained what must be done in an interview with *Live Science*: "We're trying to teach people to take pride in this animal, to understand this animal. Without them saving it and learning about it and taking pride in it, it's not going to be saved."

With all this, it might come as something of a surprise that in 2016, Peru was given the title "World's Leading Culinary Destination" by *World Travel Awards* for the fifth year running. It's also the home to no small number of trendy superfoods, like quinoa and pichuberry, which makes their cuisine healthier on

So Many Options

If frog smoothies and guinea pig kabobs haven't scared you into packing your suitcase full of granola bars and jerky for your next trip to Peru, there are other traditional dishes that might make you consider it. Like the fact that the jerky they have over there isn't made from beef or even something exotic like ostrich but from llamas. Or the bowls of roasted "big bottomed" ants, grilled grubs from the South American palm weevil, or giant Amazonian river snails, which are chopped up and made into a hearty stew. If you'd like to be adventurous, give these things a go. Maybe they'll go down a bit more smoothly if you do like the locals and dip them in clay.

average. This explains why Peruvian food is becoming increasingly popular in America (or at least California), with fifteen themed (presumably non-guinea-pig–specializing) restaurants in Los Angeles alone. No word on whether they serve frog juice. If they do, those same restaurants might have to deal with their fair share of angry protesters.

But thankfully for the critically endangered water frogs, there are plenty of people who care about them, and not just because they allegedly make men happier in the bedroom. And with a little luck and determination, we may yet again see the shores of Lake Titicaca teeming with scrotum-beasts. In a final bit of good news, the Denver Zoo was successful in breeding the very first *Telmatobius culeus* tadpoles in captivity in 2017. Hopefully it was for benign purposes and not to supply cheap ingredients for their new Peruvian-themed food court.

VIRGIN BOY EGGS

Scrambled, Over Easy, or...Oh, Good Lord!

CHINA

From rhinoceros horn to deer penis to dried gecko powder, traditional Chinese medicine can be...a little weird. Still, many people all over the world are willing to give the ancient Eastern ways the benefit of the doubt. And okay, we can admit Western medicine still doesn't hold all the answers. But if you think having an acupuncturist stick needles in your back or letting someone attach cups to your flesh means you're superbrave, get back to us once you've eaten "virgin boy eggs." Because no matter what you imagine such a food might be, we guarantee it's much, much worse. Unless of course your mind somehow went directly to "eggs boiled in the urine of little boys." Yep, that's what it is.

As much as that sounds like a portion of a federal inmate's confession transcript, eating eggs that have been soaked and prepared in pee is a tradition that goes back hundreds of years. It has to be the pee of boys, not girls. "Why?" you ask. It just is. Leave it at that. Also, it's best if the boys in question are under the age of ten, because otherwise it would be...wrong? It's a dish commonly sold by street vendors in Dongyang, a city of around eight hundred thousand people in the Yangtze River Delta Economic Region. It's not hard to find the particular stalls where they're sold; just go by the smell.

🌐 Discontinue Use If You Feel Any Wriggling

It's going to be hard to upstage the main course of this entry in terms of overall horridness, but baby mice wine might come close. This is pretty much just what it says it is—rice wine brewed with the corpses of a bunch of dead baby mice. Isn't that a bouquet to die for? It's also ancient in origin and said to cure all sorts of ailments. To make it, you drop live mice into a bottle of wine and let it ferment for a year or so until it's deemed safe for consumption. As for the taste? It's wonderful, some say—if you're the sort of person who likes guzzling gasoline straight from the pump.

To collect their golden elixir the, um, "chefs" visit the local elementary school toilets with buckets (and presumably permission from the principal). There's no proof that the eggs contribute toward your physical well-being, of course, but that doesn't stop people like Ge Yaohua, an egg vendor, from believing his cup of urine is half full rather than half empty. As he said in an interview with *HuffPost*, "They are good for your health. Our family has them for every meal. In Dongyang, every family likes eating them."

We in no way encourage you to actually prepare this undoubtedly savory morsel. But just for the record, here's how it's done.

First, soak the eggs in boy urine, shells and all, and bring the urine to a boil. (You'll notice we don't say anything here about how to get the urine.) Then take out the eggs, peel off their shells, and put them back to simmer for a full day while adding more urine as necessary. You can add herbs at this

You'll Want to Pack a Lunch

China is famous for serving foods that shock foreigners. Enough so that their cuisine was given top billing in 2018 at the Disgusting Food Museum in Malmö, Sweden. On display were mouth-watering delectables such as century eggs, stinky tofu, and barbecued pig brain. Mmmm. Pork brain. Hungry Americans will be pleased to learn that the museum has also opened a location in Los Angeles, California, where you can sample edible nightmares from other parts of the world, such as lamprey pie from England, maggot-infested pecorino from Sardinia, and Iceland's national dish: rotten shark meat.

stage if you want, but it's questionable as to whether that's going to make things better. Anyway, that's about it. Now you have salty, yellowish boiled eggs with a green yolk center. And because we know you're wondering, here's what they do to your taste buds. According to an interview with Wu Bei of the Zhang Yuming Chinese Medicine Clinic in Dongyang in *The New York Times*, "They taste a bit like urine, but not too much. It's delicious; you should try one sometime!"

You might think that eating eggs soaked in urine, even if it *is* virgin boy urine, would make your liver jump out of your body and commit suicide. But those who consume virgin boy eggs regularly are said to enjoy better blood circulation, immunity from heat stroke, and a general reinvigoration of the body. The local government has even awarded the dish the title of "intangible cultural heritage," just in case you were wondering if the cops were a little curious about the whole boy's bathroom thing. Although the "intangible" part suggests that they may be just as confused as we are why people eat those abominations.

While we won't likely be running out of eggs (or pee from young male humans) anytime in the near future, this particular tradition isn't really harmful to the environment. To the small intestine, perhaps, but not the environment. But the same can't be said for a number of other centuries-old foods and medicines that include endangered animals as the main ingredients. For instance, even though trading in tiger bones and rhino horns has been illegal for decades, in 2018, China lifted the ban for reasons that remain a mystery. The Chinese government may have gone after the ivory trade, but it is ignoring another animal that may face complete extinction in the near future because of its importance in traditional healing—the pangolin. As a side note, pangolin preparation also involves being cooked in the piddle of young boys. So where exactly should we start in terms of changing old habits and attitudes, the chicken or the egg—or the boy or the pee?

ST. JORDAN'S DAY

BULGARIA If you're a member of the Bulgarian Orthodox Church, you turn out every January 6 for St. Jordan's Day—no matter how cold it is. You may be shivering in your thermal underwear, but hey, it's a holiday that celebrates Epiphany and the baptism of Jesus. You don't want to miss that! Now, if you've ever been to southeast Europe in winter, you'll know that January 6 is a time of year that's generally far too cold to do much else other than sit inside and complain. For most people, that is. For Bulgarian men who want to increase their chances at a year filled with health and happiness (and prove their manliness), it's a chance to take part in a custom that's probably going to stop their hearts (or perhaps induce fatal shrinkage): chasing a cross thrown by a priest into the frigid water, then fighting to get it on land.

The first man to reach the holy cross and bring it to shore gets a special blessing, along with loss of all feeling in his body. That's because the dip in the water (again, we can't emphasize how cold it is) symbolizes Christ's baptism by John the Baptist in the River of Jordan. What everybody overlooks is that the river's outlet was the Sea of Galilee, which *was surrounded by a desert*! It never produced the kinds of frigid temperatures typical of a Bulgarian winter. And for those who haven't yet lost consciousness from hypothermia trying to rid their house of evil spirits, there's the "icy round dance." Because that's just what you want to do after you've been thrashing around in freezing water. There's no blessed cross with this event, just a lot of men dancing around in the water to the accompaniment of peppy traditional tunes. The women apparently have no involvement in these kinds of activities, which says a lot about the native intelligence of Bulgarian females.

On the opposite end of the Slavic spectrum, the Bulgarian tradition called *nestinari* is all about heat. On the feet. A practice similar to the Indian custom of firewalking, this version takes place in remote areas in the Strandzha Mountains, near Turkey. Its roots are pre-Christian, although it's now combined with the Eastern Orthodox celebration of Saint Constantine and Helen's Day. The brave participants enter a trance, brought about by the rhythmic beating of a sacred drum, then dance barefoot on hot embers seemingly without experiencing any

The *Kukeri*, Festival of Monsters

Another custom that aims to provide the participants with health and happiness is the folk festival called the *Kukeri*. It also has religious origins, but nothing even close to Christianity; the rituals trace back to an ancient cult. It also takes place during winter, but the truly chilling aspect has to do with the costumes worn by the performers. They put on creepy masks and animal pelts, dancing crazily in the streets. Then they visit people's homes at night before congregating in the village square to frolic and entertain young and old alike. Which all sounds like the first act of a horror movie, if we ever heard one.

pain (although this may have something to do with the lingering frostbite from chasing crosses into frozen rivers).

New Year's Eve is another occasion when chasing away evil spirits is a priority (apparently evil spirits just never take a break). Children prepare their *survachkas* (a tree branch decorated with colorful threads and other adornments). The kids then beat their relatives with their fancy sticks while reciting religious verse, with the goal of chasing away dark forces and clearing the way for good fortune in the coming year. It must feel great for the kids to get a little of their own back and whale on their parents. In return the relatives inexplicably reward them with candy. A win-win situation all around for the children, one would have to say. And by the way, should you be a guest in Bulgaria and find yourself getting smacked with sticks, coerced into frozen water dancing, and walking on smoldering embers no matter how much you protest, it's possible you didn't realize something important: Over there, nodding your

Good Luck and Don't Slip

When it comes to health and prosperity, Bulgarians have a lot of ways of seeking them. Like whenever someone needs to leave the house for an important event, say, for the first day of school, an important test, and so on. Before they go, a copper vessel of water is poured in front of the doorstep so that the challenge ahead will proceed as smoothly as the spilled water. A bride–to–be will kick over a container of water before leaving for her wedding, perhaps to represent her father's gratefulness that her water didn't break before the nuptials.

head means no, while shaking it from side to side means "Yes, I would very much like to be subjected to something highly unpleasant."

Be glad some customs haven't survived to the twenty-first century, such as the way ancient Bulgarians treated their dead bodies. If you thought splashing around in icy water was cold, what about driving stakes through the hearts of those deemed to be "bad" people, to keep them from rising from the dead as a ghoulish terrors of the night? In 2014, about a hundred of these thirteenth-century "vampire graves" were discovered near the southern border along Greece. To be absolutely sure they stayed buried, sometimes a leg would also be removed just below the knee or a plowshare driven into the collarbone.

And that's just the way the ancient Bulgarians treated the people they *didn't* like. As far as their wealthy and important people, some of them got cut in half and buried from the pelvis up, as revealed from a prehistoric archaeological dig that uncovered a graveyard dated to 4700–4200 B.C.E. If you were really special and lived during the time of the Roman Empire, you could apparently (as discovered by researchers in 2008) be treated to an interment inside your very own chariot, complete with horses and your favorite dog buried standing upright by your side. So hey, if you should wind up having a stroke from splashing around in the wintry waters on your trip to one of the most eastern countries in Eastern Europe, maybe your family could request a similar send-off from the people in charge. But the chances are probably better that they'll just be stared at for a while, followed by rapid and intense nodding.

DRINKING BAT BLOOD

The Creepiest Cure

BOLIVIA

Epilepsy. It can be really, really scary. Maybe it was brought on by the moon gods, people thought. Nah, definitely witchcraft or demonic possession. Even today some folks think there must be something unnatural behind it. And of course, that means they look for unnatural remedies. Like, for instance, parts of the Bolivian Andes drinking fresh bat blood. Uh, yeah. That'll work.

Bats can often be found for sale in Bolivian markets. As it's believed that the fresher the better, they're usually sold alive so those who believe in their health benefits can get their blood directly from the still-screeching source. The poor creatures are usually kept in horrid, cramped conditions, and their plight has attracted the attention of animal lovers like Luis Aguirre, a university professor and leader of the Bolivian Bat Conservation Program. But while he's spent years trying to both protect the small flying creatures and teach people that sucking their blood doesn't do anybody any good—not you and certainly not the bat—he still regularly receives phone calls asking if he has any bundles of live bats for sale.

Bats are pretty famous for being enthusiastic carriers of rabies, so isn't chopping off their heads and drinking their insides (which is the preferred method) just a little bit on the hazardous

The *Fiesta de las Ñatitas*

You might think giving the reverse vampire treatment to hapless bats is gruesome, but it doesn't hold a candle to the *Fiesta de las Ñatitas*. Held every November, it's similar to Mexico's Day of the Dead, but with one crucial difference. And once you learn that *ñatita* (literally "little pug-nosed one") is slang for *skull*, you'll have a fair idea of what's coming next. Instead of putting on makeup to make their faces look like skulls, Bolivians decorate the actual defleshed heads of recently deceased relatives. When night comes the people carry the heads from home (where they're kept as heirlooms) to a graveyard to express gratitude and present offerings. After the ceremonies conclude, the *ñatitas* are each returned to their private shrines, which is hopefully something a little more respectful than in between the mattress and the bed frame.

side? It sure as heck is, even though transmission of the virus via blood drinking is unlikely. Obviously just handling a panicked bat that's facing imminent execution puts you at risk of receiving a nasty bite and exposing yourself to a number of ghastly diseases. Even the alternate preparation method, in which an already-dead bat is fried whole then stuffed into an alcohol-soaked bag for future consumption, isn't really a good idea.

But not all bats carry deadly diseases. There are 133 species of them in Bolivia, and without them the mosquitoes would likely stage a coup. Not to mention the nectar-sipping bats, which are just as important to plant pollination as bees. You certainly don't have to love them or invite them into your sleeping bag for a cuddle, but hopefully one day everyone will recognize that bats are not in any way evil.

If you're tempted to treat an innocent bat like a squirming juice box while on a visit to Bolivia, remember there are many

The Silence of the Llamas

You might have a hard time feeling sorry for something icky like a bat, but cute baby llamas also get a raw deal in Bolivian traditions. Before building a new home, many people visit the *Mercado de las Brujas*, or Witches' Market, to stock up on llama fetuses. It's believed that having one around during construction will help prevent accidents and scare off evil forces. The Witches' Market is also a great place to grab some desiccated frog cadavers to boost your money–making potential (and if you stick a lit cigarette in their mouths, they *really* go to work for you). You might think that customs like these are on the wane, but reports indicate that more and more people are relying on these sorts of rituals. Which is great for the witches but terrible news for the llama population.

other options on the national menu. Sure, they might not cure your epilepsy, but neither will bat blood. So don't waste your time, and instead sample some of the local delicacies like:

- Bull penis soup. It's the national hangover cure and is usually only served on weekend mornings, when customers are mostly likely to be suffering from booze-related headaches.
- *Mocochinchi*, a local beverage that's translated as "booger juice." But don't freak out too much at that one. It's just a cold drink made out of peaches and cinnamon.

To sum up, just because something is gross and disgusting doesn't mean it's going to cure anything. Although, come to think of it, Pepto-Bismol is pretty gross.

RITES OF PASSAGE

ABORIGINAL WALKABOUTS

Turns Out You Can Make a Kid Go Outside and
Get *Too Much* Sun

AUSTRALIA Once you step out of the cities and suburbs, the continent of Australia rolls up its sleeves, spits on its hands, and gets to work on its near-unlimited number of ways to murder you. From the snakes to the crocs to the spiders to the sharks...there are all sorts of creatures with teeth, poison, stingers, or a combination of all three. The Aboriginal Australians know this, which makes the way their young men prove they're worthy of adulthood really impressive. Not only do they have to wander away from their village to brave the elements and the myriad beasts of fang and claw all by their lonesomes; they have to do it for up to six months.

This journey to adulthood is called Walkabout (or, more recently, "temporary mobility," as the former has become something of a put-down), and the Aborigine boy starts somewhere between ten and sixteen, depending on when the elders of his group decide he's ready. He'd damn well better be ready, because he doesn't get granola, a stainless steel multitool, or even a smartphone on the trek. He's got to travel by foot for distances up to one thousand miles, without a compass, and survive in the bush in the same way his ancestors did (without once being able to ask Siri if that berry he just ate was toxic or not). To survive takes years of training, listening to the advice of the adults, and understanding of multitudinous secrets passed down from generation to generation since prehistoric times. And avoiding poisonous snakes and spiders.

Walking for epic distances while having to deal with ridiculously homicidal fauna might actually not be the worst thing Aborigine teenage boys have to look forward to, depending on the value they put on their genital integrity. Circumcision for them isn't how most people envision the process—a quick flash of the knife followed by an infant crying. When a young Aboriginal adolescent's beard first starts to grow, he sits on a rock and presents his penis for someone to split with a stone knife. The length of the underside is sliced, technically called a subincision, amid what one can only assume is a remarkable amount of screaming. The penis is then flattened out on the rock to make it "lighter and more beautiful," according to Aboriginals. Finally, to make the finished product as red as

They've Been Walking for a Long, Long Time

A DNA study from 2016 found that Australian Aborigines have the world's longest-surviving culture. After convincing eighty-three of them to donate their saliva, scientists determined that they became a distinct people about 58,000 years ago (Europeans and Asians only go back 42,000 years). Splitting off from their African ancestors, they traveled east until they reached a landmass that eventually separated from the mainland to become the continent of Australia. It was an impressive finding to be sure, especially since when most people agree to give their fluids over to a professional it's usually to prove to their supervisor that they didn't smoke weed on vacation.

possible, a scarlet blossom is put into the open wound. We suppose the penis can't get any more light and/or beautiful no matter what you do to it.

In case you were wondering, this bloody circumcision ritual is still practiced today. And yes, there are occasionally gruesome mishaps. In 2014, in a remote section of the Northern Territory, three boys had to be rushed to a hospital. While most modern ceremonies have a doctor or nurse present to oversee the bladework, this time they didn't and things got… well, let's let a local ambulance driver (who also happened to be the grandfather of one of the victims) describe the scene, as reported by ABC News: "I took one look at him and he was sitting in a pool of blood…and that really hurt me, that did. I wasn't happy at all, with the whole people who done the job."

The Imperiled Penises of Perth

If the Aboriginal method of circumcision seems brutal and unnecessary, consider the fact that they're not the only ones doing it. In recent years botched cosmetic penis surgeries have been on the rise in big Australian cities like Perth, as men unhappy with the form and function of their trouser mice travel overseas to go under the knives of cheap but unregulated surgeons. As medical law specialist Karina Hafford advised during an interview with an Australian news service in 2013, "Ask a lot of questions during consultations; for example, how many times have they performed that type of surgery, or, what are their specific qualifications and training? Never be afraid to seek a second opinion." Right. So here's our opinion: "Unless it's life or death, don't let people with knives anywhere near your junk."

And the grandson further detailed his experience: "When I got cut, and I seen the blood squirting through on the wrong side, it was bad. Squirting out bad...heaps. And losing a lot of blood."

Even after walking the equivalent of a hike from England to Portugal (only with considerably more spiders) and getting their tallywackers gorily bushwhacked, some Aboriginal youths still aren't finished with their coming-of-age woes.

- The Aranda tribe has the *Alkira-Kiuma* Ceremony, during which older men toss their twelve-year-old relatives into the air and catch them, kind of like a blanket toss without the blanket.
- The Warramunga tribe has a ceremony called the *Nathagura*, or Fire Ceremony. Young men are coated in clay and showered with embers from fiery torches.
- The Arandas also have an initiation rite called the "Tooth Knocking-Out Ceremony," which involves having a (you guessed it) tooth knocked out and thrown in the direction of the participant's mother's birthplace.

Those may not sound as bad as the ones we talked about in the first half of this entry (although the tooth knocking-out doesn't sound like much of a party). So let's end things with the *Kuntam-ara* Ceremony that the Aboriginal Warramunga tribe take part in. As if having one's most delicate region sliced from stem to stern wasn't horrid enough, once the subincision is healed up a bit an elder takes a sharpened stone to reopen the urethra to "further strengthen the bonds of kinship." So far this is just a hypothesis, but it seems like if you asked everyone else on earth their opinion on such methods of "strengthening the bonds of kinship," most of them would probably vote to stick with family reunion picnics.

ANT MITTS

BRAZIL

Being a young male can be hard. You're expected to prove that you're tough enough to face the world and knock down anything it throws at you. Sometimes it's something symbolic with no risk of injury, such as the bar mitzvahs every Jewish boy must study for. With others the question is how much pain you can take to prove to the rest of the community that you're ready to be an adult. Then there's the Brazilian tribe called the Sateré-Mawé, living deep in the Amazon jungle, who make their male youth undergo a really, really painful experience: being repeatedly attacked by an insect whose sting is so terrible it's been compared to getting shot.

The bullet ant (*Paraponera clavata*) was given that moniker because being on the wrong side of its stinger is like going on a hunting trip with trigger-happy former vice president Dick Cheney. The boys who submit to this species' venomous assault don't just have to get stung once and call it a day. They must wear special mitts filled with these ants, leaving them on for up to ten minutes straight—*twenty separate times*—to prove their worth. Because, as a chief of the Sateré-Mawé pointed out, living a life "without suffering anything or without any kind of effort" isn't really any kind of life at all. A lot of people would

Don't Go Poking the...Never Mind

Another Brazilian Amazon community, the tribe known as the Xicrin, have a similar ceremony by which their young men attain manhood. But instead of stinging ants, it involves stinging *wasps*. (And you can spend some time thinking about which you'd rather be stung by: ants or wasps.) And instead of just their hands taking the brunt of the punishment, the wasps have a go at every part of their bodies. The boys must climb a tree and with nothing but their bare hands attack a nest filled with the boiling rage of winged, stinging insects. According to an article by Mariana Ibáñez, this ordeal must be endured in order for them to publicly demonstrate their "bravery, ability to withstand pain and willingness to face dangerous situations." For the wasps it's probably just a ridiculous amount of fun.

probably agree (the young men compelled to wear pain gloves, especially) that you could get this message across by making them do chores for allowance money or something like that. But hey, the ant thing works too.

Here's some more information on bullet ants, because they're responsible for the kind of intense pain that bears equally intense scrutiny. After just one encounter with a *Paraponera clavata*, you can expect twelve to twenty-four hours of suffering. Entomologist Dr. Justin Schmidt is an expert on bullet ants and after being personally victimized by these tiny nightmares, he described his experience as follows: "Pure, intense, brilliant pain. Like walking over flaming charcoal with a three-inch nail embedded in your heel. The pain is so immediate and intense that it shuts down all illusions of life as normal.

Hold On, I Got Some Frog in My Eye

The Matis tribe, which also dwells in the depths of the Amazon, has a coming-of-age tradition that's arguably just as bad or worse than getting your hands perforated by toxic ants. Insects aren't a part of this one; poisonous frogs are. To show he's ready to be a hunter, a young man must go through several different trials. First, bitter juice from a poisonous leaf gets dripped into his eyes in the belief that it will improve vision and stamina. In the next stage, called the *mariwin*, fellow tribesmen in costume beat the crap out of him. Stage three is where the frogs come in: Their toxins are delivered into the bloodstream via a wooden needle. This causes extreme nausea, dizziness, and extreme bowel movements. That last one, as hard as it might be to believe, is probably healthy, because the peptides contained in the amphibian juices may have antibacterial properties that are effective in staving off certain illnesses. Although deciding which is worse is a matter of personal opinion.

Imagine sticking a finger in a 240 volt electrical socket." Now imagine that scenario being inflicted upon you again and again and again. And again. Bet no one whines when it's time for Sateré-Mawé teenagers to get their flu shots.

For those of you who are curious about the logistics, the ants are first sedated after a brief dip in a natural calming agent. The gloves themselves, which are knitted out of strips of vegetation, are then filled with dozens of ants, each of which is woven carefully into the interior. The ants are immobilized and, upon awakening, filled with righteous rage. All the elements are now in place. The unfortunate young male experiences so much unrelenting agony that paralysis and hallucinations are common. Upon completion of the ritual, though, he'll be qualified for any and all future hunts, just so long as they don't trigger his inevitable ant phobia.

There's no real likelihood that the Brazilian government will step in and put a halt to the ant mitt custom. In fact, there are laws in place preventing any interference in the kinds of traditions that help indigenous people survive in harsh environments. We'll just have to assume that kids will be getting their fingers nibbled by ants for some time to come.

RUMSPRINGA

UNITED STATES

The Amish. Horse-drawn wagons. Old-timey no-mustache beards. Disdain for modern conveniences. They're mostly useless if you're looking for someone to repair your laptop, but they're the go-to option in states like Pennsylvania and Indiana if you're looking for sturdy wooden furniture or a shoofly pie. But there's one loophole in their strict observance of tradition. Their kids get a certain amount of time to behave just like any other "worldly" teenager. They can—and do—act like the kids you might find hanging out at the food court of the local mall. Only with more straw hats and suspenders.

Rumspringa means "running around" in German (the Amish originated from Swiss German Anabaptists). It's the time every Amish kid is given to decide what kind of life she or he wants to live. They have temporary freedom to:

- Go to the movies
- Play video games
- Dress embarrassingly
- Listen to music that drives their parents crazy

In other words, they can act just like the rest of American kids today. They get to see how the "English" (their word for the non-Amish) live and decide which path they'd like to follow. Since they haven't been baptized yet, the church doesn't get an official say in the matter. Monday through Friday, the parents are in charge. Saturday and Sunday, though, the kids get away from all the hard work and stoic humility. This seems like a pretty risky proposition, honestly, given what we know about the decision-making abilities of the average teenager in the United States (and everywhere else, for that matter).

Most Amish start their *rumspringa* at sixteen, which many recognize as a stage in the human life cycle when you make bad decisions (another one, especially for males, comes at around forty). It typically lasts for a year or two, although it

From Hoeing to Hollywood

The late actor Verne Troyer, famous for his role as Mini Me in the Austin Powers movie franchise, was born into an Amish community. The fact that he was one of the shortest people on earth could very well have been a result of the fact that the gene pool in Amish communities is alarmingly shallow. The lack of genetic diversity is called the founder effect. It's led to a lot of congenital disorders, diseases, and a high infant mortality rate. That's what you get when you put a high priority on remaining insular. But at least those Amish with inherited disabilities won't be discriminated against. As Troyer explained in an interview, his community "never treated me any different than my other average-sized siblings. I used to have to carry wood, feed the cows and pigs, and farm animals."

can go longer depending on individual choice. Many might also be familiar with this particular age range as being one during which you do a whole lot of partying. Believe it or not, Amish kids know how to party. Hearty. A sheriff from LaGrange County in Indiana described what it's like responding to a noise complaint caused by one of their massive shindigs: "Unfortunately when we do have to respond to a large gathering, party, and it's majority Amish, it's huge. Anywhere from two hundred to three hundred kids. When I say kids, I'm talking about anywhere from sixteen to twenty-two." Frequently adding fuel to the bonnet-wearing fire is a ton of alcoholic beverages and even illegal drugs on occasion. Which all adds up to what could possibly be the most entertaining episode of Cops ever filmed, if anyone ever wants to make that happen.

You might think that the vast majority of Amish youth fall prey to the siren song of wine coolers and electricity. But only a small minority choose to leave their homes and lead a life surrounded by the sins of mobile devices, combustion engines,

That's A Lot of Cloth Diapers

Just because the Amish don't like to allow outsiders into their inner circles doesn't mean their numbers are getting smaller. In fact, their population exploded from 180,000 to 320,000 between 2000 to 2017, and the trend is expected to continue. Part of the reason: The Amish have a lot of kids. They don't believe in birth control, and the average couple produces around seven babies. Plenty of free labor around the farm, of course, but it can be hard for the women who are compelled to stay home and be the sole caretaker while the men are out having the time of their lives raising barns and whatnot.

and colorful underwear. A full 80–90 percent or so (depending on the region of the country they're from) decide to stay and stick with the hard work, guinea pig husbandry, and the Lord (not necessarily in that order). So it looks like allowing their members a taste of the outside world, eliminating a life of eternal pondering on whether life would be better if they could just go see the latest The Fast and the Furious sequel, is a gamble that pays off in the end.

Amish parents are terrified at the prospect of their children becoming permanently altered by whooping it up during *rumspringa*. Not necessarily to the point where they'll up and leave the family (as we mentioned, most stick around) but to where the exposure to the modern American way of life might change things in the community and change long-standing traditions. So it's a problem—a tradition that could very well upset the apple cart carrying all the other traditions. However, unless the Amish want a corn-fed, hormone-riddled revolution on their hands, they're probably going to have to compromise. After all, how can you expect to keep a strapping young man locked in the barn with the goats when, as one teenager put it, "The English girls prefer us Amish guys because we're stronger and better built and we party harder."

CROCODILE SCARIFICATION

And You Thought Acne Was Hard on Teenagers' Skin

NEW GUINEA Looking at our ancestry, we've all got a weird uncle or a really creepy grandmother. But what about... crocodiles? The native tribes who live by the Sepik River in Papua New Guinea believe that their settlements were founded by roaming crocodiles, from which humans evolved. This belief has a practical side: To show reverence for their ancient reptilian ancestry, young men of the region get various areas of their bodies sliced with a bamboo cutting implement. This object of the ritual is, well, pain, because how could it not be? It also produces bumpy scars on the upper torso and buttocks—looking a bit like crocodile skin. Not only do these people want to honor their crocodile ancestors; they also want every generation of young men to look like they were chewed up by them.

Called the "Crocodile Men" (which makes a lot of sense), they bear small scars that are meant to represent tooth marks. The scars also look like scales, meaning they can really identify with ancient crocs. When a youth undergoes the scarification ceremony it's like he gets the wounds he received while being "swallowed" by a crocodile. This means he symbolically dies a boy and is reborn as a man. One initiate described the importance of the tradition: "The marks have many meanings for me.

The Titanic Toupees of the Huli

The males of Papua New Guinea's Huli tribe are also known as "the Wigmen." A weird name, you might think, but it's because of the importance they place on fashioning ceremonial wigs. As teenagers they're sent away to a separate location outside the village to learn how to be a productive member of the community. That's when they spend a year and a half growing their hair and making it into a massive decorative spectacle. The operation goes something like this: Three times a day the initiate's hair is wet down with holy water while fern leaves are sprinkled on top and magic spells are chanted. Bamboo is used to form the hair into a mushroom shape as it grows. Obviously, this means the kids must sleep in a certain way to keep the hair safe. They are forbidden from eating anything but food that will make their hair strong. (Now there's a diet that would be popular in a lot of countries!) Eventually there's enough to work with, and the hair is shaved off and made into a wig decorated with feathers and colored clay. If they don't mind going through the process all over again, the going price on these wigs is reportedly around $600.

I wear the marks of the ancestral crocodile. This is a power mark, a spirit, a security used for protection and connection with the totems and ancestors of my clan."

There are some villages where the young girls get the chew marks as well (they're not allowed to assume the roles of wife and/or mother until they do), but usually it's the boys. The process is basically the same for both genders, however, as they both must spend up to two months secluded in a sacred hut to complete the ritual. Outsiders are forbidden from seeing exactly what goes on, but plenty of people have heard the loud noises coming from within. The ravenous jaws of the crocodile, no doubt. Or the shrieks from the initiates once the cutting starts. Forcing clay into the wounds to accentuate the bumpiness probably also creates an atmosphere that's very conducive to screaming. Enduring the pain caused by months of symbolic reptile mauling is thought to make you both stronger and wiser. Jacob Simet, a member of the National Cultural Commission, explained its importance in an interview: "It's scientific, really. When someone is in pain, they tend to remember what they are learning. So it's kind of like that."

It should go without saying that popping a few ibuprofen at any point during the ritual isn't an option, being that pain is such an integral part of the process. After the requisite amount of lacerations are made, the bleeding young man takes a seat

Mad Person Disease

Kuru, a debilitating condition similar to mad cow disease, was responsible for the deaths of around 2 percent of the population of the Papua New Guinea tribe known as the Fore. Translated as "trembling in fear," kuru wreaks havoc on the brain and nervous system, and by all accounts is a pretty dreadful way to die. The way you contract this disease is by consuming human brain tissue, which goes back to an old and frightening funeral tradition of the Fore: eating the brains of their dead. Even though the zombie practice stopped a long time ago, the effects are still ongoing due to the disease's lengthy incubation period. Surprisingly, researchers have discovered that the brain-eating custom may have actually been beneficial, in that it helped the Fore develop resistances to kuru and other neurodegenerative diseases. So as of right now, science is on your side if you want to keep preparing brain omelets for your family breakfasts.

by the communal fire while purifying smoke is blown onto the ravaged areas. After all is said and done it does rather look a bit like the kid might have some crocodile blood in his lineage. And once everything is healed over, what's left is an impressive sort of body modification that would be the envy of any attention-seeking liberal arts college undergrad.

Shoving clay (along with tree oil) into the wounds doesn't just hurt like crazy; it also helps to prevent infection. In a further show of mercy, village elders may play soothing flute music while the flesh is getting mangled. The blood that's spilled during the procedure also serves another symbolic purpose aside from the "getting eaten by a crocodile" stuff—it represents the replacement of the blood of the boy's mother with the blood of a man. Which means he is now free from the control of his parents and can do something rebellious like get a gauge earring at the mall or something. Although that seems rather redundant.

TEETH SHARPENING

The Land of Very Few Vegetarians

INDONESIA

Ads for women's beauty products—and yes, we admit to watching them—often liken females to animals. They have the feline slinkiness of a jungle cat, perhaps. Or the colorful plumage of a tropical bird. A mouthful of sharp teeth just like the one on a shark's smiling, bloodthirsty face would sure be sexy too, right? Well, you might not think so. But the women of the Mentawai tribe in Indonesia sure do, which is why it's a tradition there to file down their teeth so they, too, can greet you with the fetching grin of a voracious hammerhead. And they don't have to pay some pricey cosmetic dentist to accomplish this task—they do it by themselves, using nothing more than some wood and a sharp piece of rock. They don't make them any tougher than that!

The Mentawai people live on the Mentawai Islands, naturally, and still exist by way of the nomadic hunting-and-gathering methods of their ancestors. The island itself is a rain forest environment, which is why they don't need to go to a city for food. It's also coastal, obviously, which explains their interest in sharks. Nowadays having your teeth filed down to resemble those fishy predators is optional, but to many, a mouthful of hazardous points is still considered the height of womanly beauty. Of course, getting your mouth to look this way is pain-ful in a way that probably makes a root canal feel like a vigor-ous foot rub. There are no anesthetics, and a stone chisel is the main tool. You can chew on a green banana to lessen the pain, but that's usually about it as far as anesthetic is concerned. Although at least it must be kind of fun tearing the banana apart with that brand-new set of chainsaw choppers.

Physical appearance is very important to both men and women in Mentawai society. If they're not happy with the way they look, their souls might flee back into the spirit world. So to keep those souls pleased the women do things like get their teeth made into points while the men get tattoos all over their bodies. Of course, they undertake these procedures with the opposite sex in mind as well. As one Mentawai women related after getting the shark makeover, "Now that my teeth are sharp, I look more beautiful for my husband, so he won't leave me." Not to mention he's probably afraid of getting mauled like a baby seal.

The old ways are important to the Mentawai, but for a while it wasn't so easy to maintain them. After independence in 1945, the Indonesian government cracked down on the tribe

Bone Sweet Bone

The Mentawai believe everything alive possesses a spirit. So they display the bones of animals killed during hunts to honor their importance. Monkeys are a popular choice. A lot of home entrances contain elaborately carved fetish panels, decorated with multiple macaque skulls. The purpose of these panels is to scare off the bad nature spirits while attracting the more pleasant ones. And presumably to freak out any foreign visitors sneaking around the village without permission.

for decades, trying to make them look more mainstream. In 1954, they tried to make the Mentawai choose whether they wanted to be Muslim or Christian. Being that they raised pigs, and "neither" wasn't an option, most of them went with Christianity. The tattoos and tooth sharpening were forbidden, as was the wearing of loincloths. Much of their cultural heritage was burned to the ground, but they managed to keep their traditions alive until the police eased off in the 1990s. Not because the government found a brand-new appreciation for Mentawai customs, but because they noticed that tourists were willing to pay a lot of money to see the tribe living the way they had for millennia.

Today the Mentawai are free to wear, pray to, tattoo, and chisel whatever they choose. But sadly only around two thousand members of their society still carry on the ways of their

Come for the *Goyang Madura*, Stay for the *Tongkat Madura*

On another Indonesian island called Madura, northeast of Java, the womenfolk also go the extra mile to make themselves attractive to the opposite sex. They're famous for a sexual technique called *goyang madura*, which involves clenching the nether regions in a way similar to Kegel exercises. Their love-making prowess has become such a selling point that the people of Madura make an impressive income selling herbal "love potions," which improve the fragrance and cleanliness of certain areas of the female anatomy. They also sell the *tongkat madura*, or *madura* stick, which supposedly returns those lady parts to their original "form." It's currently listed on *Amazon*, but it's out of stock. We checked.

ancestors. Most of them just move deeper into the forest and away from modernity. Some still live away from everybody else and worship according to the old animist belief system, although they do allow the occasional visitor to witness the way their people have been surviving for thousands of years. So if you're looking for a one-stop shop for your full-body tattooing and incisor-sharpening needs, you know where to plan your next vacation.

LAND DIVING

An Extreme Activity That's Considerably Less Silly Than Parkour

If there's one thing that says, "Hold my beer and watch this!" it's jumping off a wooden tower with vines tied around your feet. But that's just what young men in Vanuatu love to do to show their manliness creds.

The nation of Vanuatu is made up of around eighty islands in the South Pacific and is inhabited by the Melanesian people. In the southern part of one of the major islands called Pentecost, they have a coming-of-age ritual that bears a strong resemblance to an extreme hobby that many people in the West are already familiar with. You probably thought it was started by reckless college students: bungee jumping. The truth is that while British members of the Oxford University Dangerous Sports Club may have kicked off the craze in 1979, the natives of the Vanuatu archipelago were the ones who inspired *them*. The major difference is that there's no bungee involved, only vines. And there's no net waiting in case there's some mishap. Just the cold, hard ground.

The people of Vanuatu don't have tall buildings or freeway overpasses to fling themselves off of, so they build towers a hundred feet in the air to jump off. It's called "land diving." Which sounds more accurate than "bungee jumping." It's a tradition that goes back hundreds of years. Generation after generation of young boys have placed themselves at the mercy of gravity and plant matter tied to their ankles to prove they're brave enough to be called a man. Or dead, if it doesn't work out.

It's definitely dangerous, much more so than the versions you might try at some resort vacation destination. A village elder named Luke Fargo explained in an interview with ABC News: "If you come and the two vines break, it means you break your neck, or your backbones, or maybe your legs." And that's not the worst-case scenario by any means. When Queen Elizabeth visited the area in 1974, a broken vine resulted in a man dying right in front of her. However, incidents like that are just a risk that must be taken. As Fargo puts it, "It's our traditional thing, so we must do it from year to year."

The origin of land diving goes back to the legend of a woman who fled into the jungle because of the unreasonable

A Storm Shelter Ain't Gonna Cut It

Vanuatu is considered one of the most dangerous countries in the world due to the fact it's located in the Pacific Ocean's Ring of Fire and has no less than *nine* active volcanoes. When the Manaro volcano blew its top in March 2018, all eleven thousand residents had to be evacuated before they wound up like the unfortunate statues in Pompeii. Violent weather is also a frequent issue on the archipelago, and in 2015, the island called Ambrym was battered by a cyclone, an erupting volcano, and an *earthquake* within the space of just a few weeks. Imagine the devastation to the trailer parks in the region. If there were any, that is.

Don't Preach to the Big Nambas

Malekula is the second-largest island in Vanuatu and is famous for being the last place in the country where there was a recorded case of another long-standing tradition: cannibalism. But don't worry, it was a long time ago. If you consider the moon landing and Woodstock a long time ago, that is. Reportedly, a Seventh-day Adventist visited the island in 1969, presumably to proselytize, and wound up in the oven of the Big Nambas tribe (named for the large leaves they wrap around their genitalia; the Small Nambas tribe uses more modest-sized leaves). Nowadays the locale's history of man-eating is something of a ghoulish attraction, with guided tours of cooking sites that are still strewn with gnawed human bones. Since these bones may only be fifty years old or so, this is a tour during which you'd be wise to be polite.

demands of her overly amorous husband. With her husband (whose name was Tamalie) hot on her heels, she ran up a tree and jumped off, surviving the fall because she had tied vines around her ankles. Her spouse followed in pursuit and jumped off after her, but because he neglected that last step with the vines there was a loud splat, and the woman became a happy widow. To commemorate this tale of female empowerment, the women of Vanuatu decided to imitate the woman's glorious fall and began jumping from trees in a show of respect. However, the men soon decided that they didn't like what this act symbolized, and so (as men so often do) they took over the tradition. They substituted a wooden tower for the trees and began jumping for practice so they wouldn't fall for that trick ever again. Seems to kill the point of the whole legend, really.

There's a season for land diving. Specifically, the dry one during the yam harvest when the vines (called lianas) have the most pliability and are least likely to snap (a really important thing when your life depends on it). The object is to get as close to the ground as possible during the jump without receiving major contusions. If you can lightly brush the earth, you're golden. The more impressive the leap, the more good health you'll enjoy for the rest of the year. The belief is that a superlative performance can remove sickness (whereas an unsuccessful jump can effectively remove your life). You might think it's a good idea to avoid the whole thing altogether, but that would result in being called a coward and subjected to endless mockery. Presumably Vanuatu is a place where the old cliché of "If all your friends jumped off a bridge, would you do it too?" doesn't work as well as elsewhere.

There's a lot of meaning behind the wooden tower that serves as the launching point as well. In addition to being a place where you might encounter the disgruntled spirit of the previously mentioned Tamalie (jumpers must refrain from having sex, and women must keep their distance at the risk of incurring his wrath), the structure itself is full of symbolism. The supports represent legs, the midportion a torso, and the upper platform a head. The diving boards are representative of male private parts, and the lower struts are the female equivalent. So basically, you're diving off a giant penis.

As we mentioned, women are no longer allowed anywhere near the land dives. But many would probably agree that if they should happen to sneak onto the towers at night and saw off one or two of those diving boards, it would serve old Tamalie right.

COW JUMPING

At Least It's More Humane Than Tipping

ETHIOPIA

Young men in cultures all across the globe participate in tests of physical ability in order to prove to
their neighbors, their peers, and themselves that
they're ready to leave childhood behind and do
some really, really dumb stuff.

From organized sports to death-defying acts of daredev-
ilry, there are innumerable ways for an adolescent to show
the world he's ready for the increased responsibility (or irre-
sponsibility) that adulthood brings. In Ethiopia, members of
the Hamar tribe have a custom designed to accomplish this
goal that's a bit more elaborate than most. It's similar to the
famous running of the bulls in Pamplona, Spain. Only instead
of running, the bulls just stand there while a naked kid jumps
over them.

Called "cow jumping," the custom starts with a boy having his head shaved, followed by a rubdown in sand and cow
dung (to make him slippery). Strips of tree bark are then tied
to his torso to provide mystical protection as he readies himself for the main event. Fifteen or so bulls, which have all been
castrated and also smeared with dung (to ensure the event
proceeds with maximum slipperiness) are then lined up. It's at
this point that the young man can finally make his attempt to

Ethiopian Lip Plates

Ethiopia is also one of the last remaining places where people wear lip plates. The Mursi and Surma people are just about the only ones who still practice this ancient tradition, using discs that are a half inch in diameter but up to four inches in circumference. It's only the women who wear the plates in these Ethiopian tribes, the size possibly being an indicator of how many cattle were paid as a dowry. Some dispute this claim and say the reasoning behind the plates is much more complex. The women themselves aren't saying. Whatever the rationale, it's certainly a bold look that makes those nose ring–wearing teenagers smoking reefer at the bowling alley look like snively little cowards.

jump up and run across the beefy barricade without falling; he does this four times in a row. To provide encouragement, the boy's mother and any other female relatives are whipped by older men until bloody. They must not make any of the sorts of noises one normally associates with getting flogged until their ordeal is complete. If the boy fails to make it over the poop-covered cows, his family is shamed and must go through it all again the following year.

Avoiding the shame of sliding off a crappy bull's back isn't the only reason why success in cow jumping is important. This task proves a young man is mature enough to get married. (Although how many times running over a bunch of poop-covered cows is going to come up in married life, we don't know.) Moreover, he certainly doesn't want to disappoint any of the young women he encounters on the way, to whom he might offer a *bokko*. This is a small piece of wood carved into the shape of a penis (the women are required to kiss it three times and then give it back). The female relatives of the initiate also have plenty at stake, since the beating they receive is brutal enough to cause permanent scarring. On the bright side, the more visible scars a woman has, the more likely she is to attract a husband, as the wounds provide evidence of devotion to her family. How the men got to play around with livestock all day and avoid getting their backs disfigured is a mystery.

After a successful cow hurdling there is much celebration, and when everyone has finished making merry and gone home, the newly minted man can join the ranks of the Maza, or those who have already succeeded in their trials. He will live among them and eat nothing but milk, cattle blood, honey, meat, and coffee until he finds a wife. Luckily for him, the Maza are the ones doing the beating during every ceremony, so they have plenty of opportunities to meet eligible women in between cracks of the whip. There's no shortage of women to choose from, as reportedly they are so eager to prove their dedication

Just Accept the Fact That You're Going to Miss the Train

A visitor to Ethiopia can get confused very quickly because the country doesn't tell time like the rest of the world. Instead of starting a new day at just after midnight, they prefer to begin things when the sun comes up. This means that dawn, the time you're used to being 7:00 a.m., is actually 1:00 a.m. over there. Which makes a certain amount of sense, really. But that's not all. Ethiopia also has an extra month on the calendar. With thirteen months of thirty days each, it comes close to the more universally used Gregorian calendar but doesn't match up exactly, meaning at the time of this writing they're seven to eight years behind everyone else.

that they often rush the Mazas en masse, demanding to be the first to feel the lash.

With all the whipping going on one might suppose that Hamar women live in subservience to the males, but that's not exactly true. Because they tend to marry men much older than themselves, women frequently wind up becoming the head of the household and the beneficiary of all the accompanying wealth and prestige. As they are only allowed to marry once, there's little chance of some smooth-talking, cattle-surfing stranger making off with the family fortune. She may also be left in charge of her deceased husband's younger brothers should their parents have passed away as well. Which must be especially satisfying if the brothers happen to have been responsible for any of those welts from past years.

WRESTLE FOR THREE YEARS AND CLIMB A MOUNTAIN

Climbing and Wrestling and Circumcisions, Oh My!

TOGO

Climbing mountains and wrestling sound like a pretty stiff requirement for being considered a man. It's not like some countries where, basically, you just need a driver's license.

The small nation of Togo is on the western edge of the African continent, wedged between Ghana and Benin, with its southern tip touching the Gulf of Guinea. There are forty ethnic groups who reside there, and one of the oldest are the Kabye people, who make up over 12 percent of the country's population. They scratch out a living from a harsh landscape. You have to be tough to make it in the climate in which they live, which may explain why they make it so hard for young males to become adults. More specifically, if they're not good at climbing mountains and wrestling for extended periods of time, young men will be doomed to be boys forever.

The *evala* is the Kabye ritual that decides who becomes a man. It happens every July in the northern city of Kara and consists of a number of stages, ending with a weeklong wrestling competition in which boys must cover themselves in talc and engage in hand-to-hand fighting. They repeat this for three years in a row before graduating to the next phase. They don't have to win their matches, which is nice, but this is a small

The Akodessewa Fetish Market

If you should happen to be in the market for dried-out, slightly rotten elephant, leopard, or monkey heads, Togo is the perfect place to fulfill your shopping needs. The Akodessewa Fetish Market, located in the capital city of Lomé, has everything the discriminating practitioner of voodoo might require, from powdered lizard's tail to various idols and charms. The region is considered to be the birthplace of this ancient religion, where it is called *Vodun*. Don't bother checking the underside of that fetching crocodile skull that caught your eye, as the merchant must perform a ritual and consult with the gods beforehand to determine the price of the wares. Just hope they don't spend too much time listening to whichever god is in charge of bilking gullible tourists.

mercy considering all the solo mountaineering that's also part of the process. Prior to the combat portion of the ritual, Kabye boys go on a pilgrimage that requires they climb three different mountains. And not with a bunch of fancy equipment purchased at the local sporting goods store.

If the youth fails, not only does it bring great embarrassment upon his family; it also means he cannot officially be considered mature enough to be called a man. Although if you're like many among the current generation of Western youths and would rather stay home and play video games until you're in your fifties, this could be a viable option.

After completing the *evala*, participants must then take part in the *kondona*, the stage wherein the candidate gets his head shaved, climbs yet another mountain, and bangs on a gong that's located somewhere up there. But celebrating would be a bit premature; there's still the last phase of the ceremony: ritual circumcision. For those who can manage to smile after that procedure, the festivities can finally begin. Except for those who failed the mountain climbing portion and must return home with all their family members hanging their heads in humiliation for another year. Again, that might be worth it for some. Especially if they'd prefer to go through life without having someone take a knife to their privates.

If you were curious as to what the actual fighting during the *evala* entails, usually about five youths between eighteen and twenty years of age face off against five others. The main point of the event is to bring your opponent down to the ground.

The Women Warriors of Dahomey

While the girls in Togo may not have to fight to demonstrate their womanhood, females in the neighboring country of Benin have a long battle record. The nineteenth-century Ahosi warriors, referred to as "Amazons" by visiting Europeans, were famous for their combat prowess, as detailed in Stanley Alpern's book *Amazons of Black Sparta: The Women Warriors of Dahomey*: "The amazons are not supposed to marry, and, by their own statement, they have changed their sex. 'We are men,' say they, 'not women.' All dress alike, diet alike, and male and female emulate each other: What the males do, the amazons will endeavour to surpass. In every action (with males and females), there is some reference to cutting off heads. In their dances—and it is the duty of the soldier and the amazon to be a proficient dancer—with eyes dilated, the right hand is working in a sawlike manner for some time, as if in the act of cutting round the neck, when both hands are used, and a twist is supposed to finish the bloody deed.".

There are no strict rules, but conducting yourself with honor and dignity during the match is of prime importance. So sneaking in brass knuckles is probably frowned upon. For those who try to avoid participating in combat, the punishment for their cowardly behavior is exclusion from Kabye society. So maybe it's best for the faint of heart to just get in there, make like a crooked boxer who's been paid off by the mob, and throw the fight.

Kabye girls have their own initiation into adulthood, called the *Akpéma*. There's no mountain climbing or wrestling, which must come as no small relief. The girls must first take off all their clothes except for a necklace and a belt made out of shells. They are then led into the woods where a sacred rock is located. They must sit on the rock to prove they still possess their virginity. That last part is really important, and it's believed that if a nonvirgin sits on the rock she'll either immediately start bleeding or get swarmed by angry bees. Why it's bees we can't really say, but it's probably slightly better than if it was vampire bats.

LOVE, MARRIAGE, AND COURTSHIP

THE BLACKENING OF THE BRIDE

Still Less Nauseating Than Child-Rearing

SCOTLAND Scotland is a land known for confident men in fetching plaid skirts, obnoxiously blaring bagpipes, near-inedible food like haggis, and rousing motivational speeches made by blue-faced warriors on horseback who look uncannily like the original Mad Max. Oh, and also movies about heroin addicts that kickstart the careers of future Star Wars prequel actors. What the people of Scotland are *not* generally associated with is tenderness and romance. Once you learn of their pre-wedding tradition called "the blackening of the bride," that fact will remain thoroughly unchanged.

Performed in order to ward off any nuptial-ruining, party-pooping spirits in advance of an upcoming wedding day, a ritual called a "blackening" (no relation to Cajun food preparation) is inflicted upon the bride-to-be. The woman is stripped to her waist, tied to a chair, and covered in all manner of filthy, sticky substances, including everything from soot to pigs' blood (or even worse, haggis) on top of her head. During the years around the turn of the twentieth century, this unseemly pageant would also include a classic tar and feathering, along with some time spent immobilized in a pillory. Nowadays the humiliation is often accomplished by placing the woman in the back of a pickup truck and driving her around town, all to the accompaniment of a loud cacophony caused by banging pots and pans together.

Grooms aren't immune from the blackening treatment—often they, too, depending on the region, must wear the contents of a Scottish dumpster for a hat. Both women and men submit to the custom nowadays because it's believed that enduring this highly uncomfortable and public misery shows their mettle, proving they have what it takes to put up with the rigors of marriage and eating haggis and bashed neeps (mashed turnips). In other words, if you can stand having fish heads and rotten eggs dumped on top of you as you're paraded around the neighborhood, then you can handle a little farting underneath the freshly laundered comforter.

Seeing as the victims often have no idea what's to come, blackening of the bride is technically an abduction. Yet the local police force appears to take little notice, despite the

🔍 Your Maid of Honor Smells of Elderberries

Scotland is a great place to get married if you like golf courses and, of course, castles. Doune Castle might be a fun option for *Game of Thrones* fanatics, as it's been used as one of the settings to create the Starks' ancestral home of Winterfell. It was also one of the locations used in *Monty Python and the Holy Grail* and hosts an annual celebration of the comedy troupe that continues to this day. One of the castle towers would surely also serve as an ideal honeymoon destination for those wishing to examine their new bride's huge tracts of land from an elevated position.

rowdy drunkenness that often ensues in its wake. Reportedly the custom is making a comeback, as many believe in the importance of keeping such old traditions alive. Others describe the spectacle as nothing more than an organized hazing. A woman named Amber described her experience to *The Scotland Herald* in 2016: "My mum had come in one day and asked for my help moving the horsebox. Next thing I know, the doors open and twenty-five of our friends jumped out and grabbed me. I was tied up with twine and covered in mustard, custard, all sorts of different things. All I remember now is the four or five showers afterwards to try and get all the glitter and mess off me." A problem to be sure, especially considering that it's usually the future grooms who have to remove any traces of bachelor party–related glitter before their weddings.

The blackening may have got its start as a corruption of the ancient Celtic tradition of feet washing, with the accompanying pan-clanging ruckus being useful for scaring off the meddlesome Fairy Folk. While the ritual is most common in rural communities, it's also said to be catching on in Glasgow, the nation's most populous city. Perhaps it's a good thing, all things

The Alternate Way to Hurl Your Haggis

For those who want to be the best at pelting their friends with rotten perishables in advance of their weddings, the World Haggis Hurling Championship is a good way to sharpen your food–fighting skills. Throwing Scotland's most famously awful dish for distance is a custom thought to have originated in the seventeenth century, when wives would toss their husbands' lunches to them so the women wouldn't have to wade through the bogs. Watching the husbands reveal themselves by catching their disgusting lunch in their kilts must have been well worth it.

considered, since some believe it promotes humility and brings couples together through shared adversity (in the areas where both the bride and groom get despoiled, at least). Or maybe it's just an overall safer way for bachelors and bachelorettes to let off steam before the marriage without the inherent risk of waking up with a fresh bullet wound in the parking lot of a strip club.

Actually, the blackening is not in any way a replacement for debauched bachelor and bachelorette parties. The Scottish women's version of these bacchanalian bashes is called a "hen party" and involves heavy drinking, the acceptance of obscene dares, and the creation of a generalized, embarrassing public commotion. We would condemn this activity in the most strenuous possible terms if it didn't so accurately describe the average reality show on American television.

THE CRYING RITUAL

Matrimonial Moping

CHINA For most of the parties directly involved, a wedding is a joyous and celebratory occasion, filled with giddiness and pride. Not wailing like a banshee. Well, maybe for some: ex-boyfriends, drinking buddies, online gaming acquaintances, and so on. For those people it can be a bittersweet time. The parents of the bride and groom also commonly experience no shortage of melancholy at the thought of their children taking that final leap out of the nest, while the nuptial ceremonies themselves are often populated with openly weeping attendees. However, nowhere is crying more associated with marriage than in China, where the traditional custom is to blubber constantly for weeks in advance of the event.

The crying custom is said to have begun all the way back during the era between 475–221 B.C.E., called the Warring States Period. Somewhere during this time a princess was about to be sent off to another ruling family to marry a prince and become a queen. As the princess was set to leave, her mother threw herself at her daughter's feet and pleaded that she return home as soon as she could. Presumably since everyone just loves to emulate royalty, copious premarriage weeping became a widespread phenomenon. It's not as popular as it

Love and Larceny

Speaking of the Tujia people, they also practice a larceny-related custom in preparation for their weddings. The "stealing marriage" tradition involves the groom's entourage snitching rice bowls when they show up at the bride's family home to eat a meal. They deliver all the "bowls of wealth and happiness" to the groom, with the number of bowls turned over approximately equaling the amount of expected future good fortune for the couple. We're not exactly sure as to the origins of this tradition. Pirates may be involved.

once was, but some segments of Chinese society, like the Tujia ethnic group in Zhangjiajie, consider it a necessary part of the entire procedure. In fact, future Tujia brides who don't take part in the whimpering jubilee are looked down upon and run the risk of becoming a village laughingstock.

The official pre-wedding crying procedure goes something like this:

- At one month out the bride-to-be starts crying for an hour each day.
- Seven to ten days later her mother does the same.
- A week or so after that the bride's grandmother and sisters join in the tear-filled chorus, filling the house with a moaning cacophony that only ceases when the big day finally rolls around.
- During the ceremony even more sobbing occurs as the bride sings a special "crying song" especially for the occasion.

You May Experience Some Turbulence

There's great potential for crying during another Chinese wedding tradition called *naohun*, which is translated as "making turbulence at a wedding." This entails activities described as "teasing," but they sound more like something a fraternity might do to torment pledges. Things like tossing brides into water, rubbing bananas on their abdomens, and forcing them to engage in light petting with their future husband are said to be crude forms of sex education that are ancient in origin but that are encountering resistance today from modern women who find the practice cruel. So much so that many demand that a "no wedding teasing contract" be signed before they will consent to walk down the aisle.

All of this unabashed sniveling is not designed to test the groom to see if he runs for the hills with all the rampant bawling going on. Instead, pretending to be sad is meant to symbolize everyone's *happiness* at the impending union. Nonetheless, one has to imagine that this sort of wailing extravaganza can't do much for the groom's confidence.

There are a couple ways that the bride can opt to express her forced sorrow. She can do the crying all by herself or invoke the "accompanying ten sisters" clause in which female friends and family members take part in the misery fest. When the bride has company, the crying is usually kicked off by a song or a poem. The lyrics can vary, but here's a common refrain, as cited on ForeignerCN.com:

> The bird in the tree has grown up; my sister is getting married.
> Once married, when is she going back home?

Let us share the deep feeling tonight.
My sister is like a white lotus root, and no man can
resist her charm.
My sister has a sweet mouth, which every man wants
to kiss.
My sister has a pair of deft hands, good at embroidery
and weaving.
My sister is kind-hearted, respectful to both father
and mother.

In case you thought fake crying was easy, know that Tujia girls begin training for it from the age of twelve. At fifteen they get together to discuss ways to improve and engage in competitions to see who's the champion of sham whimpering. As pointless as all this may seem, the customary weeping of the Tujia takes on a more poignant aspect when you learn of the tradition's other origin story. Ritualized weeping used to be very much an expression of actual melancholy, as women used it as a way of conveying their sorrow at a forced marriage or the capriciousness of an unscrupulous matchmaker. Tujia women are completely free to marry whomever they want today, thankfully, so maybe all that vocalized misery worked. Still, we can't recommend that anyone employ this strategy when it comes to getting out of speeding tickets. Most police officers find this tactic just as annoying as Tujia grooms likely do.

CHARIVARI

FRANCE Just about anything sounds romantic when you say it in French (apart from their word for *yes*, which just sounds gross). For instance, *Charivari* sounds like a whimsical dance for lovers, or perhaps a delicious fruit-based pastry to be shared on a moonlit evening with the one dearest to your heart. But no, it's pretty much the opposite of those things. Charivari (also referred to as "rough music") is a tradition the sole aim of which is to ruin any chances of getting lucky with your new partner on your wedding night.

Once the formalities of the wedding ceremony are over and the bride and groom have successfully fled their parents and retired to their quarters for the night, drunken guests from the reception will organize to obnoxiously disrupt any potential consummation plans. They accomplish this by banging pots and pans together and otherwise loudly carrying on outside the room until their demands for food and booze are met. Even after one group of these rabble-rousers is dispersed, there's the distinct possibility that another unruly Charivari could be coming around the corner with similar demands.

You might view this tradition as good-natured fun, but it wasn't always so. In olden times, the wedding night ruckus

Le Pot de Chambre

Another unpleasant experience French newlyweds can expect to be subjected to is *le pot de chambre*. The chamber pot is an object that people used as a portable toilet in the olden days. Anyways, the tradition isn't quite as gross as it sounds—leftover food and liquor from the party gets stuffed into a chamber pot (all right, it's a little bit gross) and fed to the bride and groom to give them strength for the next few hours, with friends making a rowdy commotion until all the contents are consumed. Sometimes a piece of toilet paper is placed on top for a garnish, because the same people who find Jerry Lewis hilarious think that this a funny thing to do.

could signify a general disapproval of the union that just took place. Or it could occur outside the homes of unmarried couples to encourage them to wed or even announce that an act of adultery was afoot. Sometimes it served as a form of vigilante justice, when an angry community caused a commotion at the door of a wife-beater. Or, conversely, people might shame a man, beaten by his wife, for not standing up for himself. In some cases the proceedings could even become violent: If the people really got pissed at someone, they might sometimes forcibly remove him from his home and parade him around town to be jeered at. In England, this tradition was more commonly known as "stang riding," which referred to a long pole on which the target of a community's wrath (or an effigy of that person) was placed while bawdy songs were sung with lyrics such as:

> *There is a man in our town*
> *Who often beats his wife,*
> *So if he does it any more,*

We'll put his nose right out before.
Holler boys, holler boys,
Make the bells ring,
Holler boys, holler boys.
God save the King.

With a ran, tan, tan,
On my old tin can,
Mrs. Smith and her good man.
She bang'd him, she bang'd him,
For spending a penny when he stood in need.
She up with a three-footed stool;
She struck him so hard, and she cut so deep,
Till the blood run down like a new stuck sheep!

The end of the event could see a ritual drowning of the effigy and possibly the perpetrator himself if he didn't play his cards right.

The Death of Happiness

French bachelor/bachelorette parties tend to be grimmer than the average. They call the celebration the *enterrement de vie de garçon/jeune fille*, which literally means the "funeral for the life of the man/woman." It's not uncommon for the guest of honor to wear a fake tombstone around his or her neck and engage in other lighthearted, death-related amusements. All while the participants engage in the more familiar heavy drinking and ogling strippers. It's nice to have something in common, isn't it?

As bad as we may have made it sound, by all reports French weddings are a lot of fun. One of the main differences is that there are no bridesmaids (they're called "witnesses"). And when the groom places a ring on his bride's finger, she may return the favor by giving him a snazzy watch. The festivities themselves can take up an entire weekend, and the main attraction, surprisingly, is not on the two people uniting in holy matrimony. Rather, the focus is on the joining of two families, from kissing cousins to drunken uncles.

With such a high importance placed on family togetherness at French weddings, eloping couples who get a justice of the peace (the French equivalent of a Las Vegas quickie wedding) are looked down upon. Although with the amount of abuse they have to put up with? It's a wonder they all don't choose this option. We're not suggesting that France completely change their culture and alter the way they treat their newlyweds or anything, but they might consider doing something to address the fact that they have the third-highest divorce rate in the entire world. Maybe start by letting them enjoy their wedding night in peace?

BURYING THE BOURBON

Better Find It or the Dog's Going to Be Sick

UNITED STATES The scourge of all wedding planners who try to organize an outdoor event is the unpredictable threat of bad weather. You're counting on a sunny day, and all of a sudden the sky's full of clouds. There's a clap of thunder, and precious, lifelong memories become a soggy mess filled with sobbing bridesmaids, melted cakes, and voided tuxedo and gown rental agreements. You can't really change Mother Nature's mind once she decides a torrential downpour is in order, so relying on old superstitions is as good a plan as any. As luck would have it, there's a custom in the southern United States that aims to keep the rain away for at least one day, but it requires a great sacrifice: burying perfectly decent bottles of hooch.

Bottles of bourbon, to be more specific. The steps of this reverse rain dance procedure are as follows: First, precisely one month before the event is to take place, the bride and groom must pay a visit to the location where they are to be wed. While there, they must bury a full, regular-sized bottle of bourbon (no cheaping out with airplane minis) upside down in the earth. Note: If you're getting married at a posh country club, be sure not to accidentally dig up the eighteenth green. The brand and quality don't seem to matter much. This indicates that Mother Nature is a degenerate lush, so perhaps you may be better off burying an economy-sized plastic jug to get the most bang for your buck.

Hopefully the day you bury the bottle is a sunny one, because the weather on that day is what you're requesting for the wedding. So if it's raining, snowing, or earthquaking, maybe you should just save your money or get drunk yourself. But if it somehow works and you've successfully warded off precipitation by way of your down-home black magic, you can dig up the booze and share it with everyone present (or just get blasted in a corner alone and depressed if you're the father of the bride). While this tradition might be obscure even to some people who've lived in the South all their lives, there are wedding venues out there that suggest the custom be carried out by all their customers. Especially if the venue happens to sell bottles of bourbon, we'll wager.

The Cake Pull

While burying the bourbon is a purely American tradition, there's another Southern wedding custom that has its origins in Victorian England. Cake pulls (also called ribbon pulls) are small charms baked into the wedding cake with a ribbon left protruding. At the reception, all the single women tug at a ribbon, and the charm that's attached is supposed to tell their future in some way. For instance, if the charm is a four-leaf clover, they'll have good luck, and if it's a heart, they'll soon fall in love. Whether or not one of the charms is a cat that symbolizes the puller will become a lonely spinster living alone in a house full of felines is up to the person in charge of planning. Although it seems unnecessarily cruel.

The origin of the custom is a bit of a mystery. No one's sure exactly which state it started in, but one of the whiskey meccas like Tennessee or Kentucky seem the most likely. Some think it all began as a marketing campaign, but the more romantic story is that it came over with the first immigrants from Scotland and Ireland. Whatever the case, it makes for a fine photo opportunity, just so long as you don't mind a little mud getting on your finest Southern seersucker tuxedo. It can also be seen as a test of the groom's mettle; if he's incompetent enough with a shovel that he breaks the bottle, then how can he be trusted to get rid of the evidence when those pesky government revenuers come for the still?

Judging by the weddings we've been to, the likelihood of just one bottle of bourbon getting passed around is usually pretty slim, so there are a few things to keep in mind when attending a Southern wedding before every one of your inhibitions gets thrown out the window. A number of food items

Bottle Trees

Another bottle-related tradition from the American South is the creation of "bottle trees." Like many old-timey customs, it was started to ward off evil forces. How you make one is pretty simple—just stick blue bottles (they're usually blue) onto the branches of a tree so that it looks like Christmas at a drunkard's house. The whistling noise made by the air passing over the empty tops was believed to be caused by spirits back when glass was a new thing in Northern Africa a couple thousand years ago. The belief that those spirits could be trapped in the bottles may have been brought over from Africa by slaves. They believed that once the morning sunlight hit the bottles, the spirits would be banished, and you'd have a home free of devilry along with a festive lawn ornament.

could be on the menu that might prove disconcerting if you live north of the Mason–Dixon line. So prepare your gut for traditional delicacies like fried chicken gizzards, pickled pigs' feet, something called livermush, or even something alligator- or opossum-related. We're not saying you should expect these at every Southern wedding, but it's certainly best to be prepared. Just ask the guy who never learned how to use a shovel properly, wound up breaking a bourbon bottle, and got chased all the way up to Massachusetts by an angry Alabama mob. We're not sure if that ever actually happened, but you get the point.

PRE-WEDDING BATHROOM BANS

Better Lay Off the Fiber

BORNEO

Three days? With no bathroom? *Three days?!*

The Southeast Asian island of Borneo doesn't come up on the news cycle very often, but it is the largest island on the continent (also the third largest in the world) and boasts some of the most spectacular natural scenery and wildlife you can ever hope to see. Who knows, you might even fall in love with one of the locals should you choose to spend some quality time there. But if the object of your affection happens to be a member of the Tidong tribe, you'd better make sure your gastrointestinal system has acclimated to the local cuisine. Because if the two of you wind up getting married, tradition says that you're not allowed to use a toilet for three full days and nights. We don't mean using it to wash your hands or oil your beard—both number ones and number twos are strictly prohibited unless you want disaster to strike.

The belief is that if both the bride and groom don't both successfully hold their bowels for seventy-two hours after the wedding, terrible outcomes like infertility, the death of a young child, or divorce will surely occur. There's no honor system where this ritual is involved, either. There are a number of chaperones assigned to make sure nobody sneaks off to defile

🔍 All Creatures Great and Weird

Borneo rivals its fellow island Madagascar in being populated with some of the strangest animal and plant species in the world (in case you're looking for ways to talk yourself out of walking outside to pee). From the planet's tiniest frog to its longest insect (the incredibly named Chan's megastick, clocking in at more than twenty-three inches) to the only known double-headed nudibranch (which sounds incredibly filthy but is actually just a brightly colored slug), there's an amazing array of both flora and fauna to make you wonder if you accidentally ate the wrong mushroom during your hike. Oh, and Borneo also has glowing, bioluminescent mushrooms to further enhance your drug-free psychedelic freak-out.

the bushes or the side of a barn at night. Family members are generally the ones assigned to this task, although if you could talk your way into getting one of your friends involved, you might increase your chances of surreptitiously filling up a two-liter soda bottle on the sly. The recommended route, however, is to try to avoid getting the urge at all by fasting for the days leading up to the challenge. Also, as far as we can gather, there's no rule against flatulence. So you might as well chow down on some gas-producing foods beforehand to make sure everyone is just as miserable as you.

Not all Bornean wedding customs are gross, thankfully. Perhaps the sweetest one mandates that a groom cannot lay eyes upon his bride's face until after he has sung to her several love songs. Once his performance meets everyone's satisfaction, a curtain is raised and the ceremony can proceed. The

📍 A Diverse Island

For an island, Borneo is exceptionally diverse. In addition to the indigenous tribes in the region, there are also Indian, Chinese, and Malay influences aplenty. Most of the world's major religions are also present, so depending on where exactly you are, it can be tricky getting the local etiquette right. A majority of people who live on the island are Muslim, though, so observing the standard modesty and caution around the womenfolk is a good bet. The bonus of having so many cultures in proximity is that it seems every weekend there's a different holiday you can celebrate. If you and you beloved have some sort of fetish that involves holding in your bowel movements for extended lengths of time, you just may have found the honeymoon destination of your dreams.

indigenous folk in the northern Sabah region also have some lovely, non-colon-ravaging traditions as well. Like the one that has the couple both place one of their feet upon a stone to signify that their relationship will be as solid as a rock, after which they exchange rice balls, chicken drumsticks, and wine. Obviously the people in Sabah don't practice the whole "no crapping for an entire holiday weekend" thing, because you can just imagine.

The people known as the Sinambau Dyaks have a similar custom that's just as charming (in reference to the rock custom, not the sphincter clenching). Instead of putting a foot on a stone, they both sit on two bars of iron to symbolize the strength of their bond. A priest then hands the groom a cigar and some betel nuts, both of which are placed in the bride's mouth to make the marriage official. After that, the priest proceeds to murder some chickens to use the blood for ritualistic, omen-reading purposes. All in all, it's a very nice ceremony. Unless you have a soft spot for chickens, of course, in which case the last part kind of puts a damper on the whole thing.

The unpleasantness of the postnuptial bathroom ban seems to be the exception rather than the rule, as most traditions tend toward the romantic and sweet, both in Borneo and the rest of Indonesia, Malaysia, and Brunei (which all have a political stake in the island). Apart from the slightly frightening custom of the Sasak people of the Indonesian island of Lombok, in which grooms ritualistically kidnap their future spouses, the majority include touching symbolic acts—like the one from the Sunda Islands, where the bride lights on fire seven wooden sticks held by the groom. As described by Bridestory.com, the groom dips each stick into a jug of water, then breaks them all in half to symbolize that "fiery wrath" can be "extinguished by his spouse's gentle and soothing persona." Which seems like a pretty fitting way to end three days of holding in spicy hors d'oeuvres from the reception.

THE *GEREWOL* FESTIVAL

A Celebration of Male Beauty

NIGER

If you've ever been to a wedding, you know how all the guys ogle the bride as she comes down the aisle (and, usually, the bridesmaids). But what about the women leering at the groom and groomsmen? The vast continent of Africa contains fifty-four nations, and all of them have their own ways in which their young men and women court one another. Most are the sort of methods that everyone in the world is familiar with, from small kindnesses to the giving of gifts to using jewelry and makeup to attract attention. Usually it's the females who make themselves over with beauty products, but in the landlocked West Africa nation of Niger, it's the men who gussy themselves up with every cosmetic enhancement available. At least this is the case for the Wodaabe tribe, who have an annual beauty competition where the only contestants are male.

The Wodaabe are widely regarded as the most beautiful people in Africa, with or without makeup and regardless of gender. For this nomadic tribe, who may also at times be found traveling through Cameroon, the Central African Republic, Chad, and Nigeria, looking good is a way of life. And during their weeklong *Gerewol* Festival, the men do their utmost to win the heart of eligible females. They don't have a catwalk or put on angel wings, but that's about the only way they differ from the Victoria's Secret fashion show.

To make themselves appear taller, they adorn themselves in elaborately feathered headdresses. To appear wealthy, they wear an array of brightly colored beads. Lips are darkened with black lipstick to show off their pearly white teeth, eye shadow is liberally applied, and striking face paint completes the overall look (which is further enhanced by tattoos and highly exaggerated facial expressions). There's no swimsuit competition, but maybe they decided it was too dumb to include long before the Miss America pageant finally figured that out.

Dancing is also an important part of the festival. The painted young men move slowly in a circle while the single women approach to tap on the shoulders of the ones who particularly

The Way of *Mbodangaku*

The Wodaabe tribe is a subgroup of the larger Fulani ethnic group, which is one of the largest in West Africa. To say that the two of them don't see eye-to-eye is an understatement. The Wodaabe look down on the nonmigratory Fulani, believing they've lost touch with their roots and are ignoring important traditions. Meanwhile, the majority of Fulani believe the Wodaabe are, well, nuts and treat them with equal disdain. The government of Niger appears to agree with the mainstream Fulani assessment, with programs seemingly intended to curb the Wodaabe lifestyle of nomadic cattle herding. Although it's unlikely that they will be forever able to wander from nation to nation as they do now, most express an intense desire to follow the code of *mbodangaku*, or "the way of the ancestors."

tickle their fancy. This dance is called the *yaake*, and it can last for hours under the hot sun. A simple hat isn't enough to completely shield one from the elements, so to help with stamina, the participants guzzle a hallucinogenic drink made from fermented bark. Once the dance is over, each woman picks out a male partner with whom to spend the night, the week, or the rest of her life. Making a commitment is common but not required, so a man may wind up with a temporary girlfriend or multiple wives. Or he could lose the wife he has to someone else, which is a pretty strong incentive to lay off the fattening foods and stay pretty.

Wodaabe women believe that the most attractive physical features on a man are:

- A long nose
- Large eyes
- Dazzlingly white teeth

The makeup the men wear is designed to accentuate these features and explains why during the festival they're continuously making their eyes bulge and grinning crazily (the hallucinogenic probably helps in that regard, as well). Apart from the romantic liaisons, the *Gerewol* is a contest, after all, so the judges (three women picked by the village elders for their "fortitude and patience") have to pick a winner out of the creepily grinning assemblage. The men with the most charm, good looks, and dancing skills are declared the winners. It's probably safe to assume that the ones who look like Steve Buscemi in drag go home frustrated and alone.

The ethnic group that the Wodaabe broke off from, the Fulani, have their own traditions regarding courtship and

⦿ The Curse of the *Boofeydo*

Wodaabe women enjoy a lot of sexual freedom and are free to experience multiple partners before marriage. The culture places such a premium on physical appearance that it's permissible for a woman with an unattractive husband to procreate with a more attractive male for the purpose of creating a good-looking baby. Things get a little less open-minded when childbirth takes place, however. After having a baby, a woman is declared a *boofeydo* (translated as "taboo" or "someone who has committed an error"), which means she's suddenly a societal pariah and cannot legally speak to her husband for a number of years. Which may or not be a good thing, depending on what she wound up with after all the makeup was taken off.

marriage. Honestly, they don't sound nearly as much fun. A Fulani wedding has three stages:

1. The *sharo*. As part of it, the husband-to-be is whipped in front of a large crowd. If he cries out in pain, the wedding's off.
2. The *koowgal*. The father of the bride delivers a dowry to the groom's family. Also, the groom must prove he knows his way around a herd of cattle.
3. The *kabbal*, which is the ceremony itself. It's a rather unusual wedding ceremony, in that neither the bride nor groom have to be there.

After the knot's been tied, the bride heads over to her new home and everyone dances at the reception. It's a pretty anticlimactic ending. But the system weeds out any bachelors with even a hint of cold feet.

USABA SAMBAH FESTIVAL
Riding on Swings and Beaten with Things

INDONESIA (BALI) The Indonesian province of Bali is one of the most popular tourist destinations in the region—and unlike neighboring Australia, it's mostly not full of things trying to kill you. Famous as the home of Kopi Luwak coffee (the one made from beans pulled out of cat poop), it's also the first place on the list for many couples looking to get married or spend their honeymoons in an exotic, tropical locale with plenty of beaches to frolic on. For the permanent residents of the island, the road to marriage is a bit harder than getting all the sand out of your resort hotel room sheets. Young men participate in a yearly festival where they must mercilessly batter each other with spiky plants in order to prove to the eligible females that they're worthy husband material.

Called the *Usaba Sambah* Festival and also known as "Bali's Fighting Festival," this celebration occurs somewhere around May or June in a walled-off village called Tenganan Dauh Tukad. The melee that occurs is both bloody and ancient in origin, and it takes place during a combination of dance and fighting technique called the *Mekare-kare*. The spiky plants are pandanus trees, also known as screw pine or screw palms. These produce edible, pineapple-like fruit called drupes. The leaves, which are used as weapons during the combat, are festooned with white spikes, like some sort of photosynthesizing saw blade. Getting smacked with one is an unpleasant, puncture wound–filled experience, made even worse when a dozen or more of them are tied together to make a club.

The ritual combat itself that occurs during the festival is called *perang pandan*, and it takes place in honor of the Hindu warrior god Indra (Bali is majority Hindu). Legend states that an old king named Maya Denawa declared himself greater than any of the gods. This naturally didn't go down very well with any of the deities within earshot. So Indra vanquished the blasphemous ruler, and in honor of his victory the annual plant slapping continues to this day. Before the conflict starts, prayers are offered and participants consume a fermented drink called *tuak* to fortify their resolve. The only defense

A Foreboding Landmark

One of the more disconcerting things about villages in Bali is that they pretty much all have a highly visible, dramatic–looking "Temple of Death." The most imposing of these temples is likely the Agung Padangtegal complex, located deep within the Sacred Monkey Forest and surrounded by "guardian" macaques. Called *pura dalem*, the temples generally are situated so that they face the sea and are on the lowest available land. The entrances are lined with horrifying statues of the most violent and fearsome Hindu gods (like Shiva, Kali, Durga, and Rangda) standing on a pile of skulls. Many of them also cradle a baby, which suggests a scenario that's probably too disturbing to think about. Even more disturbing than the bug eyes are droopy breasts and mouths filled with sharp teeth, which some poor artist had to spend time sculpting.

Don't Drop That Baby

The Balinese people, like all Hindus, believe in reincarnation. Since babies are thought to have souls that just arrived straight from the body of an ancestor, they're treated with so much reverence that they're not allowed to touch the ground for three months or longer. Infants are considered tiny gods who are watched over by guardian spirits called *nyama bajang*. After the required time has passed, a ceremony takes place in which the parents undergo a purification ritual, the spirits are bade farewell, and all the child's hair is removed (as it's considered unclean—honestly, they've got a point, considering all the disgusting stuff a baby spits up on its hair and everywhere else). Only then is a baby finally allowed to make contact with the earth, at which point it also gets a name. After all that, hopefully it's not something dumb, like Chad or Trevor.

against the thorny blows are rattan shields, while the multiple lacerations are treated with potions made from saffron, turmeric, and vinegar. Serious injuries are uncommon, as referees attempt to keep things clean, while hard feelings are said to be few and far between as everyone sits together at the end to laugh and nurse their myriad scrapes and scratches. Which is pretty impressive for people who just spent hours getting pummeled by nature's version of a nail bat.

What are all the young women doing while this wanton bodily destruction takes place? They get to dress up in their best hand-spun silk finery and ride on a structure made out of swings similar to a Ferris wheel while they giggle and watch the boys smack themselves into a stupor. The rise and fall of the contraption is supposed to symbolize the relationship between the sun and the earth while also playing a part in courtship. Presumably because when the wheel reaches its apex the women get a bird's-eye view of the bachelors swinging around a screw pine maul.

Another female-only ritual held during the festival sees young women dressed in white walking in a line to a sacred spot in the forest. Once there, according to a tour guide, they weave strands of coconut fiber into each other's hair and read from holy books in order to "reinforce and cultivate self-control and honesty." We could find no part of this ceremony that included anyone getting whacked with sharpened shrubbery—which hardly seems fair.

Another practice that young, unmarried Balinese can take part in is the *omed-omedan*, otherwise known as the "kissing ritual." The translation of *omed-omedan* is "pull-pull," referring to the natural ebb and flow of positive and negative elements. This custom is relatively new, having originated about a hundred years ago when a famous fight between a male and female pig took place in the village of Banjar Kaja Sesetan. Over the years the entire island commemorated the battle by randomly grabbing and kissing anyone nearby while others doused them with buckets of water. It's said that many people find their future spouse after taking part in this event, which certainly sounds like a lot more fun than getting bludgeoned with clubs made out of stabby fronds.

KARAOKE BUSINESS MEETINGS

Sing That Journey Song a Little Off-Key Again and
You're Fired

SOUTH KOREA

Alcohol consumption has been greasing the wheels of financial transactions and commerce deliberations since time immemorial. To be a successful maker of deals you've got to be able to knock 'em back, but nowhere more so than in South Korea. Not only is the ability to down an absurd number of *soju* shots practically a requirement for business executives; so is the ability to warble a Frank Sinatra tune while inebriated.

In the capital of Seoul and just about every other city on the peninsula, when the workday concludes, cubicle dwellers and corner office holders alike congregate in downtown clubs to sing karaoke and get schnockered. It's a markedly different experience from the one businesspeople in the United States have seen since the boozy 1950s. Which is why a popular South Korean joke is that doing business in America is a "boring Heaven," while their lifestyle is an "exciting Hell."

You don't have to go far to find a *noraebang* (the South Korean word for "karaoke parlor") in any locale where there's even a smidgen of nightlife. Not only does the sauce flow freely at these establishments; other sorts of debauched vices are also readily available on the premises. There's actually a method to the bacchanalian depravity, as explained by a Korean sex

Plastered on the Peninsula

Alcohol consumption in South Korea is impressive by anyone's standard, with the possible exception of the hooch-swilling Russians. Wait, no. South Koreans actually drink twice as much liquor as Russians (although *soju*, their most common form of hard liquor, is a bit less intense than vodka) and four times as much as the average American. According to 2014 statistics, South Koreans toss back an astounding average of 13.7 shots of the stiff stuff per week. That seems like it would be enough to allow them immediate membership in just about any college fraternity that's been placed on double secret probation by Dean Wormer.

industry consultant: "When you're a man and you do something dirty and sinful with your business partner around, you share your secrets, you share trust like brothers. You can always trust your new business partner." As you may have guessed, women tend to be on the exploited side of the equation here, as it's still rare for women to succeed in the business world (although things are reportedly improving, though slowly).

The way it works is a bit different from the average karaoke night at the local tavern in Boise or Duluth. Generally you rent a room for something in the area of $5-$25 per hour, depending on the classiness or shabbiness of the establishment. After removing your shoes, you can enter and perhaps put on one of the glitzy costumes that some of them offer. Then you just choose your song from the catalog and wait while guzzling whatever drink is on hand. Some of the more modern equipment rates your singing performance, so don't go up there shrieking off-key gibberish to the accompaniment of Cher's *Greatest Hits* unless you want to embarrass your family name in front of everyone present. Also, if you're looking to refrain from tempting yourself with sins of the flesh, you might want to avoid the bars with scantily clad ladies calling themselves "helpers."

As mentioned, the social climate is changing thanks to the relentless economic development that's made South Korea's prosperity index rise to thirty-fifth in the world. Not too shabby for a country that was devastated by war less than seventy years ago. As a result, the strict, conservative Confucian traditions regarding a woman's place in society are also changing rapidly. Competing with the *noraebangs*, downtown Seoul today also has a growing number of "host bars," where women of means go to enjoy the company of attractive men for a price. Karaoke is usually included in the package, as is the opportunity to guzzle an unhealthy number of cocktails.

As prostitution (male or otherwise) is illegal, this practice is allegedly all simply about having a good time. As a typical

Dance Party Diplomacy

Howling along to Supertramp ballads isn't the only way music is important to the South Koreans. Chances are you're aware of the K-pop phenomenon. This has about the same level of annoyingness as long-extinct boy bands like NSYNC and New Kids on the Block. What may come as a surprise is that the government actively promotes popular music (along with their films and TV shows) as a way of extending the government's influence in Asia. So far the scheme has been wildly successful, and the program, called *Hallyu* (Korean Wave), seems to be poised to conquer the West via high-pitched squealing and horrendous haircuts.

patron of a host bar explains: "In regular bars the guys who drink with me have only one goal—to have a one-night stand. But I don't want that, so that's why I come here: I want to have fun." Then again, here's a take from one of the male employees at Bar 123 in the Gangnam district (remember that song with the portly fellow doing the giddyap dance?): "The guys here are pros—we know what we're doing. After talking to a girl for an hour we basically know how much money she makes and what she does for a living. We've already analyzed her personality and what she's willing to give." Yep, it seems as if the men are achieving their own sort of parity in a profession that's older than anything their clients have to groggily show up for in the morning.

SAUNAS

Get Ready to Get Steamy

 FINLAND

Finland is one of the world's chillier places—we're talking winter nights that get down to a blistering -22°F (-30°C)—and as a result the struggle to stay warm is understandably a national priority. It's where the concept of the sauna first originated, and stepping into a heated, steamy room to relax is still an important part of Finnish culture. So naturally, when doing business in this northern European nation, to be successful you must expect and be prepared to attend plenty of meetings wearing nothing but a towel (hopefully), a thin layer of shiny perspiration, and a smile.

The sauna's beginnings are rural, devised as a way for farmers to get some relief from the frigid unpleasantness of their daily duties. The women traditionally have their own saunas, presumably to get some relief from the frigid unpleasantness of the men. Sweating in an enclosed space while in the company of people you may not have ever met before has since spread to every corner of Finland, both rustic and cosmopolitan (at least as cosmopolitan as it gets over there). As odd as it may sound to the uninitiated, it appears to be working out well for them in the business arena, as Finnish industry has been steadily improving in just about all sectors.

Heated Competition

Since the whole idea started in Finland anyway, it seems only fitting that the World Sauna Championships should be held there as well. Essentially it's a test of endurance. The winner is the one who can last as long as possible in an increasingly hot and humid environment. With a starting temperature of 230°F (110°C), both the size of the prize and the unbearableness grow gradually as water is ladled onto the hot rocks in the interior every thirty seconds. If this all sounds rather risky, that's because it is. In fact, all further competition was banned after the 2010 event, during which two people sustained severe burns and one of them died.

"Naked networking" is also important to Finnish diplomacy, with a sauna installed in every one of their embassies across the globe. There's even one in Washington, DC, in case you're looking for a place to horrify yourself with the sight of semi-nude politicians. That one in particular is known for presenting "sauna diplomas" to guests who manage to endure an entire evening surrounded by birthday-suited, heavily perspiring, middle-aged Finns. And how good is this at getting diplomatic results? Well, a former ambassador to Tanzania (who went on to become one of Finland's presidents) said: "Decisions and negotiations take less time in the high heat. Sauna cools down overexcitement and melts away political differences." Which seems to be a diplomatic way of saying that everyone is on equal footing when their giblets are hanging out of a loosely tied towel.

To further disconcert guests who are novices to the etiquette of sauna, a person from Finland may perform the ritual of purification known as *vihta* (also called *vasta*) right in front of you. This involves slapping one's body with a bundle of leafy sticks from the birch tree, which is said to assist with circulation. The overall effect is to make the skin red and sore yet pleasant-smelling in an outdoorsy sort of way. Presumably it's considered good manners to remove the ticks beforehand. And for hygienic reasons, not to share branches.

Just how popular are saunas in Finland? If you thought finding room in the budget to install one in every single foreign embassy seemed a bit much, there happens to be a sauna in just about every household, which works out to around one per every two and a half human beings. And the fact that this statistic indicates that the Finns are cutting people in half and storing them in those things is another huge issue. It's hard to argue with their success, seeing as how Finland came out on top of the World Happiness Report in 2018 (a poll conducted

 Mosquito Capital of the World

Finland isn't always a snowbound hellscape. When summer rolls around the harbinger of the new season arrives: highly aggressive mosquitoes. If you thought the World Sauna Championships were a little strange, then you've never heard of the Mosquito Swatting Championship held in the swinging Lapland province town of Pelkosenniemi. The rules are simple: bludgeon as many flying parasites as you can within five minutes. So far the record is only twenty-one, which may be a frightening testament to the sturdiness of Nordic mosquitoes. If that sounds like the exact opposite of how you'd like to spend your summer, perhaps you'd be better off sticking with the Air Guitar Championships that happen each August in the central city of Oulu.

by Gallup). This may seem surprising, as the stoic Finns are known for not smiling very much. This is understandable, considering the long, cold winters they have to endure. Plus, this is the same country that invented the word *päntsdrunk*, which is Finnish for "drinking at home, alone, in your underwear." How can the folks who came up with something like that possibly be the happiest people in the world? Well, it definitely makes more sense when you factor all the saunas into it. You know, considering all the practice everyone has stifling laughter at the sight of each other's exposed inadequacies.

GIFT-GIVING ETIQUETTE

You Might Want to Write All This Down

CHINA Ever since the days of Marco Polo's journeys along the Silk Road, right up to present day, foreigners have been confused as hell about how to conduct trade with China. Especially Westerners, as differing customs and traditions can make things difficult to understand. Even presenting a simple gift can result in hard feelings all around if the proper etiquette isn't strictly observed. For instance, offering something just once is always guaranteed a refusal. Not because your gift is ridiculously inadequate (although it may be) but because the recipient is just trying to be polite. You *must* offer it again a couple more times. Otherwise, you might as well spit on the gift, rub it in a nearby pile of horse apples, and hurl it at his or her face.

The reason for this ritual is simple: The person receiving the gift doesn't want to look greedy. So just keep gently insisting a few more times, unless it's something like a horrible multicolored sweater with a panda embroidered on it. If the refusals keep coming you'll know you screwed up, so just cut it out. Also, it's considered a serious faux pas to offer a gift to someone in full view of everyone else at a business meeting. Not that you should stalk people during their trips to the toilet, but choose your moment carefully.

If, heaven forfend, you only bring one gift to a situation where many people are present, be sure to give it to the most senior person in the room. You can safely assume that this means the boss of the company, not the old man who comes in to change the snacks in the vending machine. You should always offer the gift with both hands to demonstrate respect. If somehow you manage to get a gift yourself, accept it with both hands in turn. Don't open it right away like some covetous lout. And be sure to write a thank-you email or make a grateful phone call soon afterward.

Now that you have some inkling of what to do, here are some things to avoid. First, avoid giving a gift that's sharp, like a knife or scissors. This is an unspoken way of telling the other party that you wish to "sever" the relationship. Next, remember that numbers are important. The number four is the Chinese equivalent of our unlucky number thirteen, and seventy-three and eighty-four are code for "funeral" and "having accidents," respectively. The number 250 anywhere on a gift is also to be

The Gun Is Mightier Than the Textile

The Silk Road opened up trade between China and Europe starting in 130 B.C.E. and was named for the most popular commodity the East had to offer (paper and gunpowder were also highly profitable for the Chinese, but the "Paper Road" doesn't sound nearly as good). But some say that even more important than the commercial goods that changed hands was the exposure to different cultures, religions, languages, and scientific knowledge, which were the real contributions to the advancement of the civilized world. However, whoever says that must have missed the day in class when they talked about gunpowder.

Loud and Proud

The Chinese tend to speak more loudly in public than other cultures, and they themselves refer to this habit as "the loudspeaker mentality." There are many theories as to why this is the case: Maybe it's the rapid influx of uncultured countryfolk into the cities causing everyone to yell. Or the need to be heard over a dense population with lots of traffic and construction going on. Whatever it is, it's a real phenomenon. Real enough that Switzerland began suggesting that Chinese people ride in separate coaches when traveling by rail.

avoided, as this will indicate that you're basically saying the person you're giving it to is an idiot.

Oh, you better believe that's not the end of it. Yet another gift that should be steered well clear of are women's shoes, as the word for them sounds exactly like the Chinese word for "evil." Giving someone a handkerchief, umbrella, or a pear is just another way of saying goodbye forever and is only appropriate when you're breaking up with a significant other or recently won the lottery and want to politely tell your boss to shove it. Clocks are bad luck, flowers (especially chrysanthemums and anything white) are only for funerals, as are anything that's totally black or white. Mirrors attract ghosts. Handing a man a green hat means that his wife is cheating on him, and ornamental stones from an unknown source are crawling with evil spirits.

As far as wrapping the gift goes, you can do the whole ribbons and bows thing without repercussion. Unless of course those ribbons and/or bows are black, white, or blue, which all symbolize death. As does writing a person's name in red ink. So unless you've found yourself embroiled in some triad initiation ceremony, stick to the colors red (lucky), pink, yellow (both symbolize happiness), or gold (wealth and prosperity).

There are more things to avoid, but there's only so much time in the day. Just remember that you're in a place where giving someone something as innocuous as a rock can get you in trouble, so don't get too creative. Just head to whatever the Chinese version of Hallmark is. If whatever you get costs exactly 250 yuan, be sure to peel off the price tag.

LEFT HANDS AND SHOE SOLES
Southpaws Beware

UNITED ARAB EMIRATES Little things can cause great offense when dealing with people from other lands. What might seem perfectly innocuous to you may be the same as calling someone's mother a promiscuous goat, depending on where you happen to be. For instance, in Western societies using your left hand to perform everyday functions like eating, drinking, handling objects, or touching a person wouldn't raise any hackles. But in some nations of the Muslim world, such as the United Arab Emirates, using your left hand indiscriminately like that is the equivalent of exiting the bathroom without handwashing, picking your nose, examining a dead rat you just found on the street, and then offering a hearty handshake to initiate your business meeting.

The teachings of Islam hold that the left hand is unclean and should only be used for...personal hygiene. We're not talking about toothbrushing, mind you, but the kind of hygiene that involves sitting on porcelain and thorough wiping procedures. So you can kind of understand why someone from the UAE might find it a little off-putting when the person who wants to do business with them uses that particular hand around people and foodstuffs with carefree abandon. Okay, now that you have that protocol fresh in your mind, you can take a load off and get the meeting underway. Just don't cross your legs so that the sole of your shoe points toward the person you're dealing with, because that's considered just as filthy and degenerate as the left-hand thing.

Modesty is very important in the UAE, as in other Muslim countries—not just for women, but for men as well. Obviously, prancing around in public with a tube top and cellophane bike shorts is inadvisable, but so is wearing anything but a dark suit with a conservative tie to a business meeting. If your clothing is inappropriate for the occasion, don't worry because someone will tell you. If it's too unseemly, don't be surprised if you're told to return to where you keep your luggage and change. Likewise, women should take care to dress conservatively, with a dress hem that's below the knee, no aspects that could be considered in any way "revealing," and colors that don't have the word "neon" in front of them. The wearing of a head

Mind Your Ps and Qs in the UAE

Causing minor offense in the UAE isn't the only thing to worry about there; it's also a place where it's easy to get yourself arrested if you're ignorant of the local ways. Many of the things that can get you into hot water with the authorities can be avoided merely by using a little common sense. You're in the Middle East, after all, so men should avoid public displays of affection with the opposite sex and not stare at females. Swearing and pointing at or taking pictures of people at random can also attract the attention of local law enforcement. And wearing your thong bikini while walking down the streets of Abu Dhabi is just asking for trouble.

covering, or hijab, isn't a requirement for non-Muslim women, but it's a good idea to keep one on hand just in case you find yourself near a religious site.

None of this information should be particularly surprising to anyone who's familiar with Islam, and we're not saying these customs are weird. But now that you know what to avoid, here are some things you might be surprised that you totally *can* do. You can be disorganized during your appointments without too many repercussions, snack away during meetings, and pick your teeth after a meal. You can also be loud in conversation, but don't interpret that as a license to be rowdy. Disorderly (and especially drunken) behavior will put you on the fast track to a graybar hotel (jail, to the uninitiated).

Businesspeople who are used to getting things started early on Monday mornings should be aware that the work-week in the UAE begins on Sunday. Friday and Saturday make up the weekend there, with Friday being the traditional day of rest. That should be easy enough to get used to, but what might take a little more time for Westerners (who are used to a rather large personal space requirement) is the custom of

It's All about the *Wasta*

The Arabic word *wasta* is roughly translated as "clout" or "pull" and refers to the UAE custom of using connections and influence to accomplish your goals. It's kind of like the English word *cronyism*, but not quite. It has nothing to do with a person's merit or job performance but rather with nepotism and who you know. A foreign traveler can't do much about the nepotism part, but this system of net-working and favor-trading must be kept in mind for those who want to grease the wheels to financial success.

kissing and nose rubbing that serve as common forms of greeting. You should make every effort not to panic when someone invades your personal bubble, as it's just a way of being friendly. Backing away is considered rude. Women do the nose rubbing thing to one another as well. However, as you may have guessed, when you're a man you should avoid at all costs going up to random women and attempting a nose rub. Unless you'd like to spend the remainder of your trip trying to arrange for someone to send you bail money.

CLOSE TALKING

Bubbles Will Be Burst

 BRAZIL Americans on average want at least four feet of space between themselves and strangers, between one and four feet for friends and family, and a single foot for a special few. That's a lot of space, but then the United States is a big country. But not all societies are so squeamish about pressing the flesh, Brazil being a prime example (those swimsuits they wear should have provided a clue). So if you're trying to do business in South America's largest country, it's important to keep in mind that getting close and personal will probably happen frequently. When it inevitably happens, you should make every effort not to wince and shrink away into a maintenance closet.

You can practically guarantee that there will be a nonhostile invasion of your comfort bubble when interacting with Brazilians. It's not that they're being overly forward or impolite. Rather, the custom there is to stand close. They also make a lot of physical contact during conversation; germaphobes will have panic attacks. But to back away as if you've been approached by a leprosy victim will cause the person you're dealing with to take great offense (unless they actually do suffer from a skin disease, in which case they're probably used to it), and any

For the Love of the Gol

As passionate as Americans can be about their favorite sports teams, it's nothing compared to the Brazilian love for soccer. *Futebol* is practically a religion over there, and they've placed their own particular stamp on the game.

- Brazilian players tend to be more flamboyant
- Standout athletes are put on par with A-list movie stars
- The emotional investment of the fans is without equal (there's also an occasional bit of violence involved)

Employers even have to have a TV set up during World Cup matches if they expect anyone to show up for work.

hope of securing a lucrative agreement will become as scant as the bikinis on Ipanema.

Despite their willingness to close the distance between themselves and someone with an indeterminate level of hygiene, Brazilians are typically very concerned with cleanliness. Especially of the dental variety. Brushing one's teeth four times per day is the norm, and it's not uncommon to see someone brushing her teeth at work. Such is the national obsession with oral immaculateness that restaurants commonly hand out mouthwash after meals. Also, as living in the immediate vicinity of the Amazon rain forest can make you rather sticky, Brazilians are also known to shower multiple times (summertime being the peak season, of course), with many people showering four times in a day.

No Boob Zones

While there are certain liberties taken during Carnival, it's illegal for women to run around topless on the beaches of Brazil. Barely-there bikinis are allowed, as anyone who's ever been to Rio de Janeiro on a gawking expedition can attest, but full-frontal nudity will get you in just as much trouble as waggling your business around in a mall in Saugatuck, Michigan. After all, you're standing underneath one of the biggest Jesus statues in the world (the almost-one-hundred-foot-high Christ the Redeemer), so try to have a little respect.

Even more so than the constant cheek kissing to say hello (always start on the right to avoid accidental headbutts), visitors doing business in Brazil may be taken aback by the vast amount of vacations Brazilians take. How do these people get any work done? It's common for workers to get thirty days of paid time off per year, along with no less than eleven official holidays. Expect them to vacation between December and February, since that's when summer happens there. However, should you ever have to grant days off for a Brazilian employee, don't signal your assent by making the "okay" sign with your thumb and finger. Because in their culture that is basically the same as flipping them the bird. Unless you're in the mood for denying their request in the most jerkish way possible, in which case it's entirely appropriate.

There's at least one Brazilian custom that America really should consider adopting. No, not the tiny bikinis, but the one about being on a cell phone while in a bank. It's illegal to talk on one while people are conducting financial transactions, and violators are subject to stiff fines. It's not because talking loudly on a phone in such a setting is so incredibly rude (even though it is). The rule is actually for the phone-owners' benefit, as it's intended to prevent them from being robbed as they exit while distracted by their mobile device. A similar law says you can't enter either public or private premises without first removing your motorcycle helmet or other such head covering. Presumably exceptions can be made for firefighter helmets, hazmat masks, and beekeeper veils, but in those cases there are clearly bigger problems afoot.

Finally, while Brazil is home to some of the world's most delicious foods (churrasco and an acai bowl, anyone?), before attending a business lunch, steel your gut in preparation for one of the most heinous abominations to ever be classified as a beverage: avocado smoothies. Also used as an unlikely ingredient in shakes and ice cream, avocados are widely considered a fruit in Brazil, while Americans associate it more with something to dip their tortilla chips in. The best advice we can offer is to add enough honey and whatever else you can find to sweeten things up enough to where you don't wind up re-creating the pea soup scene from *The Exorcist*.

ENTERTAINMENT

THE FATAL *BASANT* KITE FESTIVAL

Death from Above

PAKISTAN

Sure, you've probably been to a few kite festivals. Adults and children alike show up at the local park to participate in the high-flying whimsy or just lie on a blanket, drink a couple of beers, watch the colorful airborne splendor, and fall asleep. Pakistan also has a fun-filled yearly event that celebrates the joy of kite flying. Only theirs is slightly different. Every time it occurs lots of people die.

The Punjab province of Pakistan is home to the historic *Basant* Kite Festival, which takes place in late January or early February (depending on where it falls on the Hindu calendar) and marks the start of spring. It's been going on since the nineteenth century, when kites were first introduced to the area. Lots of people, from the common folk to the Maharaja and his family, ran outside, yelling, "Let's go fly a kite!" Kite flying became so popular that some people described it as an "epidemic," where "less educated or illiterate laborers" would lose all sense of propriety and descend into fighting with both kites and fists. And then things got really bad. People began attaching glass to their twine to convert their kites into deadly weapons. After nine people were killed in 2005, the authorities banned the event. But of course people still fly their murder kites in spite of the law.

"Kite flying has become a risky sport," stated the chief of the government's Emergency Management and Research Institute (and master of understatement) in 2016, after a hundred people were sent to emergency rooms in Gujarat with kite-related injuries in the month of January alone. The situation gets so risky that during the two days of the festival, hospital admissions consistently shoot up by 10-20 percent. That's not counting the victims who get a one-way ticket to the morgue. Yet no matter how many bystanders meet their maker as a result of this "fun," hard-liners maintain that the strings must be fitted with hazardous attachments. How else can you cut the line of your opponent and win the game? Hasn't anyone heard of acceptable collateral damage, for crying out loud?

Amid all this mayhem and carnage it's easy to overlook the other attractions at the yearly fair, where you can also enjoy

The Terror of the Twine

Humans aren't the only victims of this regional sport; enthusiasts in neighboring India kill or maim thousands of birds every year with glass- or metal-coated string during their celebrations of Independence Day and other events. Officials in Delhi passed laws so that it's now illegal to buy, sell, or store specially treated twine, called *manja*, upon penalty of 100,000 rupees or five years in jail. Lord knows what the charge is if you're caught with *manga*, as we imagine the penalties for possessing tentacle porn are equally severe.

local cuisine, carnival rides, and more or less normal activities. Even the kites themselves aren't always out to claim the blood of the innocent. In 2014, many of them bore a public service message to be vigilant against the H1N1 swine flu virus. Although to be honest, it might have prevented more tragedies if they advertised Kevlar turtlenecks. But sometimes the danger isn't limited to just those who don't pay attention to the whereabouts of swirling, deadly twine or who foolishly poke their heads out of their car's sunroof. Sometimes the metallic string gets tangled up in overhead electric cables, leading to spectacular electrocutions. Or sometimes they just cause a short circuit and leave everyone without power for a few weeks.

The government's been thinking of lifting the ban, and as of this writing it appears that the *Basant* Kite Festival is set to make a comeback. After what we have to assume was much heated deliberation, the Punjab government gave the green light for festivities to kick off in early February 2019. This is welcome news for the kite and string industry, whose profit margins have suffered a terrible blow since the 2005 restrictions

Loose the Toys of War!

Violence and kites have always gone hand in hand. When the ancient Chinese invented the devices, they weren't intended to be toys but were designed instead as weapons of war. Used as fire starters, reconnaissance gatherers (you can calculate distances with the string), and instruments of psychological terror, kites have even been a part of highly destructive (yet somehow delightful) bombing campaigns.

were enacted. Not as terrible as sudden decapitation via glass-encrusted wire, but you get the idea. At any rate, the area expects a resurgence in commercial activity and rupees in the billions as a result of an influx of hotel and restaurant customers. Sadly, if everyone abides by all the safety regulations, it looks like it will be the turn of the bandage, antibiotic, and suture industries to suffer.

PALIO, THE WORLD'S DEADLIEST HORSE RACE

Esoteric Equestrianism

ITALY

Most people consider the sport of horse racing a noble and dignified affair. It's been called "the sport of kings." At the Kentucky Derby the wealthy get to strut around in silly hats and sip mint juleps while tiny men whip their pampered and expensive equines to victory. Or the Dubai World Cup, where sheiks in pristine white robes make wagers that exceed the national GDP of Micronesia. In Italy, however, there's a horse race that prides itself on being down and dirty. Very down and very dirty. Down in the sense that it's common for multiple riders to violently faceplant in the mud, and dirty in that cheating and betrayals are as much a part of the proceedings as the guy who has to come in afterward with a shovel and a bucket to collect all the horse apples.

Rightfully considered one of the most dangerous sports events in the world, Italy's Palio di Siena race happens twice every summer and includes plenty of features to make the competition more exciting. Things like abnormally small tracks, a "no saddles" rule, and crowds that can most charitably be described as "overly exuberant." This all contributes to annual multi-horse pileups and mangled jockeys, as frequent as the rude, multitudinous chin flick gestures we assume the riders

Definitely a Long Way from Gladiator Days

Just like a lot of other folks, the people of Italy like fast horses. However, their love for creatures of all types seems to be exceptional, at least based on some of the news stories that have emerged in the past few years.

- **In 2017, Italy banned the use of all animals in circuses**
- **The year before they provided sanctuary for victims of the exotic animal trafficking trade**
- **They even rescued a dog from the clutches of Danish authorities who wanted to euthanize it merely for being born a member of a "dangerous" breed (Argentinian Mastiff)**

It is indeed heartwarming to see a nation care so much about the innocent beasts of the world. Almost as nice as back when they used to treat their pet lions by feeding them delicious Christians on a regular basis.

make at each other during the course of the race. As far as rules go, there's really only one: Don't mess with the reins of another jockey. Otherwise, pretty much anything goes. Kicking, biting, spitting...whatever. And the human participants can get away with a lot of stuff too.

Using a whip made of dried bull penis and dressed in wildly colorful uniforms, riders are known for flailing their opponents just as much, if not more, as their mounts. It's definitely not an easy race in which to be a jockey, and this is compounded by the fact that jockeys only find out which horse they'll be riding four days before the race. On the bright side (for the owners, at least) a horse can win by crossing the finish line even if its

Italy Gives the Boot to Fishbowls

Here's further proof that Italians adore animals, and especially their pets. In 2005 the capital city of Rome, as part of the Fish Empathy Project, placed a ban on round goldfish bowls on the grounds that such artificial habitats provide insufficient oxygen and can affect a fish's eyesight. Furthermore, a national law mandates that all dog owners must walk them regularly, and those who abandon dogs (or cats) can face jail time. Which must be a pretty hard thing to explain while you're trying to look tough in the prison yard while surrounded by murderers and such.

rider is still down in the mud collecting his teeth somewhere else on the track. If all this savage pageantry seems eerily familiar (even if the closest you've ever been to Italy was the Jersey Shore), it might be because the Palio di Siena served as the backdrop for the opening scene of the James Bond movie *Quantum of Solace*. There never was a better time for Daniel Craig to use a stunt double.

The Palio is said to have started back in 1656, because someone believed he'd been visited by the ghost of the Virgin Mary, which naturally called for a celebration. Or maybe it began in the thirteenth century as a training exercise for Roman soldiers (who rode atop water buffalo and donkeys instead of horses). If it was neither of those two things, it could have been a fun way to let off steam after the Grand Duke of Tuscany outlawed bullfighting more than 350 years ago. Whatever the true origin, the main aspects that appear to have survived to the present day are brutality and lawlessness. Under-the-table bets and unscrupulous double dealing abound before the race commences, with no official consequences for those who engage in the kinds of activities that would get someone banned for life in most professional sports. The entire spectacle, according to some observers, "illustrates the Italian soul." Which seems rather a rude thing to say, really. Especially considering that Benito "Il Duce" Mussolini was a superfan of the sport.

To celebrate their victories, those who perform well suck on pacifiers (no, really) and sip from wine-filled baby bottles, as acting like an infant is believed to be symbolic of rebirth. But for the jockey who manages to avoid getting kidnapped or getting his horse drugged (both of which have happened in the past) and manages to place first, the prize is proudly waving the banner of the team (called a *contrada*) they represent. And bragging rights, of course, but that's about it as far as compensation goes. But presumably he gets to keep the bull penis, to do with it what he will.

WIFE CARRYING
To Have and to Haul

FINLAND Finland is not a nation renowned for its appreciation of whimsy. We think of its people as dour, taciturn curmudgeons, citizens of the Land of a Thousand Lakes. Even that nickname sounds exasperating, quite frankly. Can you imagine being put in charge of naming all of them? So how can this Northern European country have come up with a sport where husbands have to run a race while carrying their wives on their backs? It sounds way too frivolous for the average Finn. Could there be some grave, distressing origin story behind all the tomfoolery? Well, of course there is. Actually, there are three. And they're all based around a serial criminal named Herkko Rosvo-Ronkainen, Finnish for "Ronkainen the Robber."

The legends are as follows: Ronkainen the Robber and his merry band of murderous, rapacious thieves had a habit of running off with the food and women of every village they found themselves near. Hence, men carrying wives are emulating the great robber. The next legend says that the way Ronkainen and his men acquired wives was by stealing them from every village they found themselves near. Which sounds pretty similar to the first legend, just with a little more commitment. The third legend involves less kidnapping but an equal amount of larcenous behavior: Ronkainen trained the members of his gang to carry heavy bags (sometimes containing live animals) on their backs to facilitate the efficiency of their pilfering, and the likely reason women got involved was to slightly lessen the possibility of bite wounds. Eventually one or any combination of all three tales of wanton hooliganism evolved into a pastime that now has its own category in the *Guinness World Records* and that has spread to other areas of the world to include other parts of Europe, Australia, North America, and Hong Kong.

Some subtle strategy is required for those who wish to be successful at *eukonkanto*, which is the Finnish word for "wife carrying." Even apart from the risky gambit of asking (as nicely as humanly possible) one's partner to keep her weight within competitive parameters, competitors must choose which transport strategy they wish to employ.

The Happiest Nihilists on Earth

As we mentioned previously, Finns may not be the most grim and sullen people on Earth. In fact, the Finns were ranked number one in the 2018 World Happiness Report, moving up from the fifth-place slot they held the previous year. Finland was also ranked one of the safest places to live according to the 2018 Travel Risk Map, which assesses things like a nation's current state of medical facilities, overall security, and road safety. So either those stereotypes about them being eternally grumpy have been wrong all along, or they've just gotten really good at faking test results so foreigners will stop asking silly questions and leave them the hell alone.

Some of the different carrying styles include:

- The standard over-the-shoulder fireman's carry
- Piggyback
- The extraordinarily saucy "Estonian-style," in which the woman wraps her legs around the man's neck and grabs hold of his chest from the back

How to negotiate and overcome the various obstacles on the course, such as water pits, logs, and sand traps, must also be taken into consideration. Figure out which tactics make for a better performance, especially with so much on the line. Because if you come in first place in the race, you get the glorious prize of your wife's weight in beer.

Surprisingly, the women clutching on for dear life during the race do not in fact have to be legally married to the men

The Air Guitar World Championships

A relatively recent tradition is another event that seems completely out of character for the Finns: the Air Guitar World Championships. Although it does make more sense when you take into account the Finnish people's unnatural fascination with heavy metal music. Beginning life as a sideshow at the 1996 Oulu Music Video Festival, it's since gone on to become immensely popular in its own right. Today there's an entire network of national air guitar competitions that includes twenty countries across Europe, Asia, North and South America, and Australia. Because this is information you cannot live without, the winners in 2018 were Nanami "Seven Seas" Nagura of Japan (earning the gold), American Matt "Airistotle" Burns (silver), and Canadian Dana "Dana-Saurus Rex" Schiemann. Although there were no Finns in the top three, at least they had a legitimate reason to be stereotypically glum.

hauling them around. The woman can be anyone's wife. Or nobody's wife. Apparently the only requirement is that she was, is, or could theoretically be a wife at some point in the future. She must be at least 108 pounds as well as seventeen years old or more, because carrying a toddler around in a wife-carrying contest would be both cheating and weird. As far as equipment goes, the man is allowed to wear a weight belt, and the woman can strap on a safety helmet. Presumably the man protects his own head in an emergency by using his rider as an improvised airbag.

It's not just the fleetest of foot (and sturdiest of lumbar region) who wins a prize during the *eukonkanto*. There are also awards for those who show up wearing the best costume and for the couple who is deemed "most entertaining." That last one doesn't seem too hard, as long as you and your partner are willing to sacrifice your dignity (what's left of it after entering this contest). So perhaps the best idea is to spend less time working out and put in more effort on your outfits. Then all you have to do is flop around in the mud and scream a lot to get yourself a woman-sized mug of free beer.

PUNKIN CHUNKIN'

Farm-Fresh Weaponry

 UNITED STATES Pumpkins may not be the world's most popular vegetable, but they certainly get their proper due every late October when they're carved into spooky jack o' lanterns and baked into pies. Not to mention how the dreaded "pumpkin spice" gets infused into every product imaginable, including cream cheese and chili. In addition to being an edible squash, pumpkins are also effective as artillery ordnance. Just ask the "backyard engineers" who've been launching them skyward since 1986 at the World Championship Punkin Chunkin'. As you can see, these folks are clearly more about science than spelling.

The weaponry used to launch the pumpkins can vary. Some entrants prefer old-fashioned trebuchets and catapults. Others go the more modern route by deploying air cannons. For those cannons, the emphasis is on "air," since the use of explosives and/or electricity is forbidden. Besides requiring a bit more ingenuity on the part of the competitors, this also protects the integrity of the ammunition as well as onlookers. As far as some other rules go, the pumpkins have to be between eight and ten pounds. Their journey into the blue yonder must be facilitated only by the sorts of contraptions that, according to *HowStuffWorks*, use "springs, rubber cords,

If You Can't Take It with You, Make It Rain

Pumpkins aren't the only things falling from the sky in Delaware. When a bait and tackle shop owner named Leonard Maull passed away in 2012, his last wish was to show his appreciation to the members of his hometown community in the city of Lewes. His novel way of accomplishing this was by requesting in his will that a helicopter be rented to unload $10,000 in small bills from high onto his friends at the Lewes Harbour Marina. It was certainly a much kinder gesture than if he had decided to dump his shop's remaining supply of nightcrawlers.

counterweights, compressed air, or any other device that uses the stored power of one human being." So any smartasses who show up from the Large Hadron Collider project looking to sneak some particle acceleration technology into the mix are just plain out of luck.

For those who want to get involved in Punkin Chunkin', there are plenty of divisions to choose from. These include:

- Air Cannon
- Female Air Cannon
- Centrifugal
- Catapult
- Torsion
- Trebuchet
- Human Powered
- Centrifugal Human Powered
- Youth Air Cannon

- Youth Catapult
- Youth Trebuchet
- Youth Human Powered
- Youth Ten & Under
- Theatrical

To win in any of these categories your pumpkin has to land farthest away from the source, except in the theatrical category. For that one the crowd votes on whose presentation is the most entertaining. Every team gets three chances over three consecutive days. Those who have an eye on the all-time record will need to beat the 4,536.57-foot distance set by American Chunker, Inc. That outfit beat the record previously held by Young Glory III, who beat the distances set by Second Amendment Too, Hormone Blaster, and team Big Ten Inch.

There are four evil geniuses allegedly responsible for coming up with Punkin Chunkin': John Ellsworth, Trey Melson, Bill Thompson, and Donald "Doc" Pepper. Back in the 1980s, Ellsworth owned a blacksmith shop, and the group got their kicks tossing anvils around. After a while they got tired of this and were inspired after reading an article about a physics class that used pumpkins in a science experiment. Their brainchild eventually became an event featuring over one hundred teams, all competing for the top spot. Until 2014, when logistical issues forced a cancellation. And 2015, when insurance companies refused to provide coverage. But after addressing all concerns the championships resumed in 2016 to much fanfare.

By 2016, the World Championship Punkin Chunkin' had attracted enough attention that both the Science Channel and the Discovery Channel planned shows centered around the proceedings. However, one of the vegetable-flinging

📍 Launching This Pumpkin Might Count As a Weapon of Mass Destruction

New Hampshire is another location on the East Coast of the United States that's made an important contribution to North American pumpkin history. Because it's there that the world's largest specimen was recorded in 2018. Steve Geddes of Boscawen showed up at the Deerfield Fair with an absurdly ginormous entry weighing in at 2,528 pounds. Which is somewhere in the range of a MINI Cooper hatchback. It was a case of very close but no cigar as far as the world record goes, however, as the reigning champ is a 2,624-pound pumpkin from Belgium. That weighs as much as a MINI Cooper hatchback with a fashion model in the passenger seat.

pneumatic cannons experienced a malfunction that caused metallic shrapnel to seriously injure a female bystander. The television shows hastily pulled out, the legal fallout was inevitable, and the entire future of the event seemed in doubt.

There is some good news on the horizon, however: The organizers plan to revive Punkin Chunkin' in 2019. Their press release states in part, "The past two years have been the hardest on our non-profit organization, both mentally and financially, following the unfortunate incident in 2016 and the ensuing litigation. However, the board remains committed, and our membership is still intact. It is this type of commitment and loyalty within our organization that compels us to move forward." So all they need at this point is a site with enough land available willing to take a chance and a little luck bestowed upon them by Melonicles, the Roman god of gourds. Which isn't something that exists, but probably should.

DEADLY *DAMBE*

The Most Fun You Can Have Without a Nail Bat

 NIGERIA

Around the world, people continue to find new and innovative ways to beat the crap out of each other. A multitude of nations have their own unique, traditional forms of martial arts. Aside from the obvious like Japanese karate, Chinese kung fu, Brazilian jiu-jitsu, and American boxing, there are plenty more that are not as widely recognized. While the formerly obscure Israeli Krav Maga may be gaining in popularity, most people haven't heard of combat arts like Malaysian *silat* or *Eskrima*, the national sport of the Philippines. Even though both of those disciplines are considered to be among the world's most dangerous forms of dispute resolution. But if sheer brutality is what you're in the market for, there's nothing like the martial art practiced among the Hausa people of Northern Nigeria. The one where you beat your opponent's head in with a punching glove covered in glass.

Believed to have begun among professional animal slaughterers and butchers, the sport known as *Dambe* has been around for centuries. Guilds from one area would challenge those from other parts of the country and fight during harvest celebrations, naming ceremonies, and funerals (which seems appropriate) while bloodthirsty spectators cheered from the sidelines. *Dambe* was also once used to train men for war and served as a way for them to earn wives as a victory prize. Today, however, combatants participate for the honor and prestige (not to mention the hefty payday).

A *Dambe* match typically lasts for three rounds. In order to be declared the winner a fighter must beat the man opposite him to a bloody pulp. The violence results in the sport having its share of detractors. Among them is Femi Babafemi, an amateur boxing coach, who described how he felt about the ruthless melee on display: "It's too brutal. Those that are doing it are really endangering their lives." But it could definitely be worse. Remember that bit we mentioned earlier about the gloves covered in glass? That part is actually illegal now under the modern rules, but not so long ago the fighter did indeed dip his gloves into a mixture of resin and broken bottles. Which might explain why "killing your opponent" is an expression used in *Dambe* circles when one fighter has bested

Lutte Traditionnelle

Another Hausa martial art, one that also can be found in other African nations including Senegal, Niger, Burkina Faso, Togo, and the Gambia, is called *Lutte Traditionnelle* (French for "traditional wrestling"). Like the Japanese sport of sumo, the goal is to force your opponent out of a circular ring (although you can also win by making the other person lose his footing and fall down, or by making him go down on all fours). Also like sumo, there's a lot of male nudity. The main difference between *Lutte Traditionnelle* and sumo is that the African athletes tend to be more muscular and trim than the Japanese leviathans. Which, you might think, would make the sight of unrestrained glutes slightly less unsettling to the unprepared observer.

another in combat. Mostly because it probably wasn't always just an expression.

In American boxing, the glove softens the impact of the blows. Even without the glass, a *Dambe* glove serves the exact opposite purpose. In fact, it's not really a glove at all but a piece of cloth covered in tightly wound cords that acts as a bludgeoning instrument. Fighters only wear one of them, on their dominant hand, and refer to it as their "spear." The nondominant hand, called the "shield," remains unencumbered and is used for grabbing, pushing, and whatever else you need to do. One leg is often wrapped in chains and can provide both offensive and defensive capabilities, while the other leg is primarily

 Mr. Poison Shares a *Musangwe* Story

Yet another vicious, centuries-old African martial art is called *Musangwe* and comes from the other end of the continent in South Africa. Essentially it's the sort of bare-knuckle brawling glamorized by mustachioed nineteenth- and early twentieth-century fighters in Western nations. A match only ends when one of the fighters can no longer continue. But when nobody gets knocked out and neither party is willing to concede, things can get a little out of hand. One of the fighters, Tshilidzi "Poison" Ndevana told a story to *The New York Times* of one such occurrence: "The longest fight was in 1998 and lasted five days," Poison said. "They just kept fighting for around two hours each day. Neither fighter wanted to give in. The spectators had to call the village elders to come in and convince them to make it a draw." Poison didn't mention whether or not there was a rematch, or if the two became completely dedicated to nonviolence and opened a florist shop together.

used for kicking. It's about as close as you can get to gladiatorial combat in this day and age without having a fat emperor getting fanned with palm fronds and giving a thumbs-up or thumbs-down from the stands.

The warlike nature of *Dambe* carries over into just about every part of the sport, with the area in which fights take place called a battlefield and with one of the two major fighting organizations called Dambe Warriors. Bleeding to death in the dirt like a soldier in the trenches isn't as much of an occupational hazard as it used to be, thankfully. Doctors are regularly present during matches now, and referees make sure things don't get *too* gory. These steps are necessary if that organization we mentioned, along with its counterpart the Nigeria Traditional Boxing League Association ("The Dambe Warriors" is a much less cumbersome title), have any hope of legitimizing and effectively monetizing their livelihood. Because if you show up at an insurance agent's office and mention even a quarter of the stuff involved in this sport, they'd more than likely make an excuse to use the bathroom, shimmy out the window, and peel off into the sunset.

CAMEL WRESTLING

The Hardest Part Is Getting Them Into the Unitards

TURKEY

Wrestling—as anyone who's aware of Dwayne "The Rock" Johnson and Hulk Hogan knows quite well—is going strong today. And it's been around for a while. It was one of the main events in the very first Greek Olympic Games, and art from ancient Egyptian (and Babylonian) times displays examples of moves that are still in use today. There are even 15,000-year-old cave drawings in France depicting the sport. But large men in spandex jumping off the top of ropes and yelling a lot isn't the strangest sort of wrestling out there. That prize goes to the nation of Turkey, where they make their prized camels do it.

Camel wrestling is a traditional and extremely popular sport in Turkey, with a certain type (known as Tulu camels) bred specifically for the task. It probably dates back to around 2,400 years ago, when nomadic tribes depended on the beasts for survival. And for slapstick entertainment, apparently. Today the competition usually takes place during the camel mating season, when the males are much more likely to be belligerent toward one another.

Turkey Loves Oil Wrestling

Turkey has another wrestling exhibition that takes place every year, and this one doesn't involve a single dueling dromedary or even a brawlin' bactrian. Oil wrestling dates back to the days of ancient Sumer and Babylon and is currently Turkey's national sport. As such, it's taken very seriously. Each competitor puts on a pair of leather pants called a *kisbet*. The object of the sport is to grab the pants and throw the wearer off his feet. This is made more complicated by the fact that, as the name of the sport implies, everyone is greased up like a cheap slice of pizza.

There are a number of different categories a hostile humped camel can compete in, and three ways to win:

- By making an opponent fall
- By making an opponent turn tail and run
- By making an opponent scream

The reason being, we assume, that the wail of a camel in distress is such a heinous assault on the ears that it makes a screaming goat video on *YouTube* sound like a Pavarotti aria.

The prefight parade features the contenders prancing (or as close to that as a camel can manage) around in colorful blankets, pom-poms in their tails, and other assorted gaudy adornments. They have names appropriate to their bellicose natures—a *New York Times* reporter listed a few in 2000, after attending an event, recording noms de guerre such as "Thunderbolt, Falcon, Destiny, Black Ali, and Jackal." Fans of the

A Cautionary Camel Tale

Camels aren't just good for riding across vast distances and being forced to fight for our amusement. They were originally domesticated for milking. The same qualities that allow camels to survive in harsh environments came in very handy for the inhabitants of such places who wanted a nice glass of lactose. Camels also have a surly streak, which is probably what prompted the Turks to make them wrestle in the first place. So, no matter if you have one of these mammals around for riding, milking, or whatever else, be sure to treat it well so you don't wind up like the guy in Rajasthan, India, who had his head bitten clean off by his camel in 2016, after leaving it out in the sun too long.

primal conflict begin assembling well in advance of the opening ceremonies, and bets are placed. The owner of a successful fighting camel enjoys great prestige in his hometown. When the day of reckoning comes and his churlish contestant enters the combat arena, his friends and neighbors grow tense with anticipation as they wait to see if his camel can win the coveted carpet. Oh, yeah, that's what you get when you win, by the way. A nice carpet. Well, not *that* nice, but more on that later.

Camel wrestling spectacles are usually not attended by the top levels of society and are more a diversion for the working folks. As one fan noted to the *Times* reporter, "You don't see fancy high-society types at a camel fight. We're the real Turkey, the real people, the backbone of this country." The owners of the camels, however, do have to possess a reasonable amount of disposable wealth as the cost of breeding and training doesn't even come close to being covered by the couple hundred bucks or so they receive for agreeing to participate in an event. And neither does the prize given for winning, as one trainer explained: "As for the carpets, they're all machine made and not so good."

There may be little money to be made, and the carpets might kind of suck, but those who raise and train camels to wrestle professionally don't do it for financial reasons. They keep the tradition going for much more exalted purposes, like pride, honor, and the satisfaction of making the other guy's camel scream. Also, as the trainer mentioned earlier puts it, "It's about keeping something alive that was given to us by our grandfathers and great-grandfathers."

So unless animal rights activists somehow convince the Turkish government that the whole operation should be shut down, it appears camel wrestling is here to stay. Honestly, PETA probably has much better things to focus their attention on. Injuries to the animals are rare, and their existence does not appear to be in any way cruel. Camel wrestling isn't like cock fighting or other blood sports where the audience cheers as creatures tear each other limb from limb. It's more like a Three Stooges short where the violence looks bad, but nobody actually gets hurt and everyone laughs. And Curly is a goofy-looking beast of burden named Thunderbolt.

FINGERHAKELN

One, Two, Three, Four, I Declare a Diagnosis of
Post-Traumatic Arthritis

AUSTRIA

Sports that revolve around the pushing or pulling of fingers (not to mention the one involving flatulence) might sound like something only children would engage in. Games like thumb wars and rock–paper–scissors are mostly popular among the world's preadolescents. But in the Alpine region of the Central European country of Austria, finger games are regarded with deadly seriousness. Finger wrestling games, to be more precise. And rather than being some harmless kid's pastime, their finger games can leave the competitors' hands mangled and maimed for life.

Called *Fingerhakeln*, the Austrian (and southern German) sport of finger wrestling began as a form of Teutonic conflict resolution years ago. Since then it's evolved into an organized test of wills and digit strength for which men train as strenuously as any Olympic event. The championships are held in Bavaria each year, and the regulations are as follows: Two men (it's always men, and the wearing of lederhosen appears to be mandatory) who are referred to as "hookers" sit across from each other at a sturdy table and place their fingers into a leather strap. Any finger can be used, except for the thumb (the pros tend to stick with the middle finger, however). Once the overseeing official gives the signal to start (*"Beide Hakler, fertig, zieht!"*), they each try with all their might to pull their counterpart across the table. Needless to say, it's not the most mentally taxing of athletic endeavors.

Earlier we briefly mentioned the possibility of disfigurement. Today participants train their finger by squishing tennis balls, lifting small weights, and doing single finger pull-ups. Long-time *Fingerhakeln* contenders are known for being able to perform impressive feats of strength like supporting their entire body weight with a single finger. Regimens also include exercises designed to increase pain tolerance. This is a necessary task, as nasty dislocations and broken fingers are commonplace, and those who compete for years may wind up with hands that look like they've spent decades jamming them underneath the wheels of passing semitrucks. As one thirty-year *Fingerhakeln* enthusiast named Emil Raithmeier

🌐 You'll Be the Grandest Lady in the Krampus Parade

Another example of how the Austrians of the Alpine regions enjoy making children's activities unpleasant is their Krampus processions. At Christmas-time, townsfolk don hideous masks to celebrate the half-goat, half-demon (also known as Perchta) who, legend says, follows St. Nicholas around to punish the youngsters who have been naughty. Naughty enough to be tormented by a half-goat, half-demon. These monster parades, in addition to teaching toddlers that the true meaning of Christmas is terror, have become lucrative tourist attractions. And presumably provide a great place for horror movie special-effects artists to hone their skills.

explained to a reporter from BarBend.com, "You need to have thick calluses on your fingers, otherwise the injuries are very painful. Thin skin rips off easily, tendons tear, and joints dislocate. You have to make sure to use magnesium powder to reduce friction—this is the only protection that's allowed." What also helps is having a girthy digit, as a fat finger is said to allow you to better get ahold of the leather strap.

Like weightlifters at a bench press dealing with a risky amount of pounds on the bar, *Fingerhakeln* matches require spotters (called *Auffängers*) so that neither the victor nor the defeated go hurtling over the table or backward into the beer stein-holding crowd. There is no women's division, as far as we're aware. In fact, females, while not exactly prohibited from attending a *Fingerhakeln* competition, don't ever seem to be present in any abundance. It's believed this may be a holdover from the olden days, when finger wrestling was a way for farmers who were pursuing the same female to behave as childishly as possible. There are divisions that separate competitors

The Smell of Romance in the Air

Some areas of Austria even manage to somehow turn the process of courtship into a spectacle that most people would find off-putting. In a few rural parts of the country, young women engage in a ritual dance with apple slices tucked into their armpits. Once the slices are nice and sweat-soaked, she hands them out to the potential suitors she finds most desirable. If the young man is of the notion to reciprocate the romantic interest, he will eat the apple. Presumably wiping the sweat off is considered rude, and it would probably be even more offensive to the woman if the apple was later taken on a hunting trip and used to attract badgers.

according to their height and weight, however, just as in other combat sports. These include light, middle, semi-heavy, and heavyweight. There are no flyweight or featherweight classes, a situation that may have something to do with the massive amounts of lager being consumed.

Fingerhakeln is unlikely to overtake sports like football, soccer, or even curling in terms of international popularity. And you're probably not going to find a single participant who's not either Austrian or German. But up in the Alps it's still going strong and looks like it will continue to do so, unless some busybody makes a fuss about all the men in the area being rendered useless because of degenerative arthritis.

BUZKASHI

Grabbing a Gutted Goat for Glory

AFGHANISTAN Although its top athletes have been attending the Olympic Games since the terrifying one hosted by the guy with a weird mustache that was held in Berlin in 1936, Afghanistan isn't known for producing world-class sportsmen. But although the nation has never really funneled much currency toward sports, at least one of its citizens managed to secure a couple medals in the recent past: Rohullah Nikpai won the bronze medal in Tae Kwon Do in 2007 and 2012. Cricket is reportedly Afghanistan's most popular pastime, so maybe if that ever becomes an Olympic sport, the country can garner a few more. And if the committee somehow approves their *traditional* national sport, the one where riders on horseback fight over a dead goat, they'll probably get the gold every four years for the next century.

Buzkashi, which roughly translates as "goat grabbing," is a grisly pastime that's taken place on the plains of Central Asia for centuries. It's a lot like polo, only there are no mallets, and the ball is a headless, disemboweled goat. The object of the game is to secure the cadaver and deliver it across the finish line, all while the other mounted competitors try to take it by force. Winter is considered *buzkashi* season, and it's usually not hard to find a game going on most Fridays. It's been an

Sometimes a Bronze Medal Is Good Enough

Being the only Afghan recipient of any Olympic medals worked out well for Rohullah Nikpai. Born in 1987 and raised in a refugee camp during the country's civil war, he was inspired by watching kung fu movies on television and decided to dedicate his life to martial arts. After he won the bronze in 2008, he became a national hero, and the president at the time, Hamid Karzai, gave him a free house, car, and other luxuries that Nikpai could only have dreamed up while living as a victim of war. His response to the accolades was both impressive and selfless: "I hope this will send a message of peace to my country after thirty years of war."

immensely popular spectator sport since anyone can remember. It's a lot like how some people plan their week around watching a Sunday football game, only instead of a pigskin getting tossed around it's—as we mentioned—a mutilated goat.

In the old days, *buzkashi* wasn't just a way to have fun at the expense of an eviscerated barnyard animal; it was also a way to prepare for war. Equine sports were often combined with martial preparedness in the days of rampaging mobile forces like the army of Genghis Khan. It makes perfect sense, as few other such events can as effectively test a man's courage and guile. The winner of a *buzkashi* match, respectfully known as a *Chapandaz*, receives a similar amount of local adoration as Cristiano Ronaldo does from the soccer-loving community or NFL quarterback Tom Brady does from the New England area. *Buzkashi* champions are pro athletes just like any other, with a lifetime of devotion to their sport under their belts. And possibly a little gore wedged in there, left over from an ill-fated billy goat.

The Mourning of Muharram

Religion is another aspect of Afghan culture that can get a little bloody. During the first month in the Islamic calendar, many Shia Muslims take part in the Mourning of Muharram. This event is meant to commemorate the death of one of Muhammad's grandsons in battle. Part of this ritual (which occurs in other areas of the Middle East as well) includes men whipping themselves with chains that have razors and/or knives attached and the use of swords to purposefully create head wounds. This is done to demonstrate grief over the passing of the martyred Husayn ibn Ali, with the profuse public bleeding earning condemnation from some clerics, and a hearty endorsement by others.

There's actually a considerable amount of strategy in a sport about fighting over a slippery carcass. And also a lot of equipment required. If the *buzkashi* rider doesn't want to spend the rest of his life limping or concussed, he needs to strap on:

- A helmet
- A thick coat
- Whip shin guards and padding
- Kneepads
- A good pair of leather boots

Plus, the boots need to have special heels that lock into the saddle equipment so the rider can lean off to the side for more efficient goat snagging.

The whip is only used for horse encouragement, in case you were wondering. Even though some matches can last as long as several days, using it to take out aggression on the other riders is frowned upon. Speaking of the horses, they also require extensive training and can be a lot more expensive than you might expect (unless $50,000 was the number you had at the top of your head). Some local warlords have even been known to keep equines worth upward of $100,000 in their stables. These costs are not considered outrageous, as Mohammad Sharif Salahi, the president of the *buzkashi* federation in Balkh province, explained to a reporter from *The Hindu* newspaper: "Only one horse in a hundred stands a chance in *buzkashi*. Everything depends on their strength and their resilience. They are trained to respect and behave calmly, but if you let go, this one eats the others." We'll assume he didn't mean that literally.

As you might surmise, those kinds of price tags tend to be prohibitively expensive for the average Afghan. So to offset the cost, a rider might partner up with a wealthy person or a successful business for the type of sponsorship deals you see in other sports. Theoretically, if you have a horse purchased with money from the Spinzar Cotton Company in Kunduz, you better not let the Afghan paparazzi catch you wearing a coat made by Ghazni Wool in Kabul.

THE *SONGKRAN* FESTIVAL WATER FIGHT

Getting Nice and Squishy for the New Year

 THAILAND

The Thai tradition known as *Songkran* seems like too much fun to be a religious festival. While most demonstrations of faith are solemn affairs with strict rules, this ancient custom seems more like the sort of thing that sweaty children might invent in the middle of July. Although its origins reach back further than seven thousand years, during a period in humankind's history when religion was something that few would associate with the words *relaxing, mirth* or *carefree abandon, Songkran* is essentially a citywide water fight.

Conveniently, *Songkran* takes place during the summer months, so it's not very hard to convince people to come out of their homes to partake in the action. There are no restrictions in terms of how you can deploy your H_2O ammunition, as everything from buckets to water guns and balloons are considered within bounds. Even the trunk of an elephant can be used as a means of dispersal, and it's hard to imagine anything more unfairly overpowered than that. Perhaps a water cannon of the sort used in riot control, but if you see one of those being used, it's probably safe to say the fun times are over. Anyway, the widespread war of wetness begins in the morning and lasts until well into the night, when everyone finally retreats peaceably to their residences to get some dry air onto themselves.

The word *songkran* itself is Sanskrit for "shift" or "to pass into" and refers to the changing position of the sun in astrology. Technically this shift happens every month, but the one everyone celebrates falls nearest to the coming of the new year, likely because that's generally considered by just about all cultures to be an optimal time to party. It's also the period when the sun moves from Pisces the fish to Aries the ram in the zodiac calendar, if you're the sort of person who cares about that kind of thing. All told, the celebration lasts for three full waterlogged days. April 13 is when it all begins and is referred to as the *Maha*, or "Great," *Songkran*. Day two is *Wan Nao*, the transitional day between the old and new year, while the

King's Cup Elephant Polo

Thailand's national sport may be Muay Thai boxing, but if you like your competition on a grander scale (and with more tusks and trumpeting), you really can't beat elephant polo. Which is just like regular polo, only with plucky pachyderms. And much longer mallets, presumably. The King's Cup Elephant Polo event occurs once a year in Thailand, with two more taking place in Nepal and Sri Lanka. Kind of like the Triple Crown of elephant contests. Rather, it *used* to occur. Unfortunately allegations of animal cruelty caused sponsors to withdraw and brought the King's Cup to a halt in 2018. However, organizers have vowed to make changes to the way the elephants are treated in the future, so hope springs eternal that it may one day rise again like an immense, wrinkly phoenix with a hose on its face.

The Phuket Vegetarian Festival

Thailand is a nation where everyone is free to worship as they please, although the yearly Vegetarian Festival contains some elements that many foreigners might wish were banned from public view. This nine-day event takes place in the province of Phuket (be careful of how you pronounce that in mixed company). What's notable about it has nothing to do with meat-free diets or vegan lifestyles. In order to transform themselves into mediums capable of contacting the gods, celebrants skewer their cheeks and other body parts with knives, swords, and other sharp implements. Deaths have been known to occur at the festival, but remarkably not due to blood loss. The last fatality resulted from the indiscriminate use of fire-crackers, which might be even harder to have to witness than the face stabbing.

final day on April 15 is called *Wan Thaloeng Sok*, meaning "to begin a new era." One must imagine that the hangovers after this kind of new year's bash are pretty intense, since most seventy-two-hour drinking binges don't also include the added unpleasantness of being damp.

As for why the celebration proceeds in the particular way it does, we have to go back to the olden days when Thai citizens had a very specific way of offering their appreciation for the Buddhist monks in their midst. Early traditions required that the monks be offered gifts and food. As well, holy water was to be poured over them in a purification ritual. After this was complete, the people would collect the water and pour it over each other in the belief that it was blessed. So, as the years went by and one thing led to another, we now have an annual national holiday where entire towns engage in open water warfare.

If you happen to be a tourist visiting during *Songkran*, step one is to buy a waterproof bag (something that's readily available at the local markets, believe it or not). And if you choose to participate in the festivities by buying a water pistol (or something with more firepower), be sure not to shoot people in the face. Using water that's neither frigid nor boiling is also a good rule of thumb. Yet another important bit of protocol, for those looking to avoid getting pummeled by an angry crowd, is to refrain from firing at babies, the elderly, or monks. Unless they're the ones who initiate the hostilities, in which case all's fair, as they say. Just be sure you have a witness as to who shot first.

FESTIVAL OF THE STEEL PHALLUS

Not Quite As Weird As You Might Think

JAPAN

Any festival featuring a giant phallus was going to make it into this book. Japan's tradition called *Kanamara Matsuri* is not a sporting event, nor does it occur strictly for the amusement of the masses. It's more of a secular form of worship, really. But you can't deny its entertainment value. On the first Sunday of every April, the industrial city of Kawasaki (located just south of the capital city of Tokyo) hosts a celebration of male genitalia. Locals and distant travelers alike fill the area, forming a procession around a colossal pink and metallic facsimile of the most sensitive area of the male anatomy and providing an escort as it's delivered to a special shrine. A "penis-venerating" shrine. Welcome one and all to the glorious majesty that is the Festival of the Steel Phallus.

The celebration is spiritual in addition to being urological. The Kanayama Shrine, long popular (at least since the Edo period of 1603–1868) among prostitutes who sought divine protection from sexually transmitted diseases, became the site of the festival in 1969 (the Summer of Love in the United States, coincidentally). While the shrine is also said to be of assistance for those praying for marital harmony and smooth pregnancies, these days it's all about the penis. Due in no small part to the large number of tourists who arrive to gawk at the unabashed glorification of the *chinko*. Which is the Japanese word for…you know.

Like many old traditions and customs, this one arose from a legend. Buckle up, because this one's a little intense. So, as the myth goes, a demon fell in love with a woman and naturally he decided to possess her vagina. Being a very jealous demon, he proceeded to bite off the penises of the first, then the second man she was to marry. Not wishing to subject any further paramours to this gruesome fate, she enlisted the aid of a blacksmith, who hammered out an iron penis. This gambit succeeded in tricking the demon, who broke his teeth on the blacksmith's creation. Thus the demon fled from the woman's nethers, everyone lived happily ever after, and today thousands of people celebrate by parading a gargantuan dingus through the streets.

South Korea's Haesindang (Penis) Park

Neighboring South Korea has its own special location that's dedicated to the glory of the gonads. Haesindang Park (also known as Penis Park) is on the east coast of the republic, within the town of Sinnam. It's remarkable for its large number of phallic statues (and even a lighthouse shaped like a penis). The most interesting thing about this location is the legend that led to its existence. As the tale goes, a man put his virginal bride on a rock out in the sea as he left her to go to work for the day. After an unexpected storm caused her to drown, the fishermen of the area were suddenly unable to catch anything and blamed the dead woman. And so the man urinated in the water, which caused the fish to come back. Why? Because his wife, being still a virgin, was so happy to see male genitals that she lifted the curse and allowed the fish to return.

The Naked Man Festival of Okayama

After getting your fill of penis at the *Kanamara Matsuri*, a fitting follow-up could be to attend a *Hadaka Matsuri*, or Naked Man Festival. These events happen in various locations across Japan, with the largest taking place at Saidaiji Temple in Okayama. It's relatively unchanged from a ritual that began five hundred years ago; a priest at the temple tosses talismans into a crowd of thousands of men. Naked men. Actually they're all wearing skimpy loincloths, but close enough. To be one of the few who manages to acquire one of the talismans is considered fantastically lucky, so the competition to locate one among all the flesh pressing is sweaty and fierce.

Make that multiple dinguses. Recently the number has actually grown to three, with all of them serving as portable shrines. The first is the metal one for which the festival gets its name (and to commemorate the vagina demon's extremely bad day). The second is made out of wood and is old and twisted. And since 2017, there's been a third, designed and carried aloft by a group of transvestites calling themselves "Elizabeth Kaikan" after a Tokyo salon that caters to cross-dressers. Who can say what the future will bring, but as the old saying goes, "the more (penises) the merrier," we suppose.

Inevitably, food vendors and souvenir purveyors are out in force during the festival, all of them putting an erotic twist on things like popsicles, candles, and whatever else you might expect to find if porn star Ron Jeremy operated a roadside gift shop. But despite all the flagrant flaunting of male dangly bits and turgid trouser mice, the atmosphere isn't one of filth or perversion but rather of happiness and good-natured frivolity. There are plenty of children on hand, and nobody finds that unusual because it's less about what people consider the "dirty" aspect of sexuality and more of an excuse for people to simply have a good time. Also, nowadays the main focus of the event is a noble one indeed—to raise both money and awareness for HIV/AIDS research. And with fifty thousand people now showing up to watch the procession take place, that sure is a whole lot of penis. Uh, we mean awareness.

FOOD

NIGHT OF THE RADISHES

Don't Miss the Nativity Salad

MEXICO

Noche de Rabanos is Spanish for "Night of the Radish." It may sound like a low-budget horror movie, but tourists don't have to worry about giant radioactive tubers terrorizing the populace. It's a Christmas tradition, actually, with a little Halloween thrown in for an extra dash of holiday flair. And as you may have already surmised, radishes are heavily involved. Although they're not for eating.

Just as Americans like to carve scary faces into pumpkins every late October, artisans in Oaxaca, Mexico, enjoy taking a knife to deface vegetables on December 23. But instead of limiting themselves to crooked smiles, triangular eyes, and such, the creations on display during the Night of the Radish are much more intricate. They can represent anything from a nativity scene (the most popular, unsurprisingly) to the wild animals that populate the countryside—and hopefully some awesome combination of the two where the lambs and donkeys in the manger are accompanied by venomous snakes and toothy crocodiles. Actually, that might get someone in trouble, so we would advise against commissioning one of those for your holiday centerpiece.

Come for the Anthropomorphic Radishes, Stay for the Ants

The Mexican state of Oaxaca is one of the most biologically diverse areas in the country, in terms of the number of animal species. So in addition to wildlife–themed radishes, there are also lots of local culinary options such as rabbit mole, grilled intestines, and winged ant tacos.

The very first official *Noche de Rabanos* took place in 1897, after the mayor of Oaxaca, Mr. Francisco Vasconcelos Flores, recognized how popular the practice of artistically mutilating radishes had become and set aside a day to engage in such activities. As legend has it, radish carving started when two Spanish friars gathered up some of the goofier-looking radish specimens after a particularly bumper harvest and brought them into town, billing them as "demons" and "monsters." Since radishes had only recently been introduced to the area by European colonists (along with a bunch of fancy new diseases), they were still something of a novelty and attracted a lot of attention. Merchants got the bright idea of carving them into entertaining figures to entice people into their shops, and things just snowballed from there. As much as anything can snowball in Central Mexico, that is. Soon everyone from young children to lonely farmers got involved in making radish dioramas, radish people, and radish critters.

Nowadays the celebration is more popular than ever, with prizes and even diplomas (as an incentive to "keep their talent and heritage") handed out to the winners of three different categories (the best carved radish wins a grand prize of 12,000 pesos). The radishes themselves are larger than the normal variety and are not intended for human consumption. So any hope of everyone in town frolicking inside a giant bowl of salad to end the festivities probably isn't in the cards.

If you were worried about getting bored at seeing radish after radish cut up to look like the baby Jesus, rest assured there's plenty of other stuff. There's also an "Immortal Flowers" competition and an event where people make figures out of corn husks. While religious themes dominated the entries of the past, today one will see Mayan imagery, characters from movies, and other pop culture references among the obligatory plant-based Virgin Marys.

According to reports, lines to view the radishes can stretch for miles, which might make the hour you spent standing around at Disney World just so your daughter could spend five seconds with a teenager in a Princess Elsa costume seem a lot more reasonable. So if you want to gawk at the misshapen red tubers yourself, you might want to arrive early. Ideally, five days early, so you can catch the feast of the patron saint of Oaxaca, Our Lady of Solitude. And what's this celebration all about? you ask. Well, according to another legend, in 1620, a mule driver was traveling through Oaxaca on the way to Guadalajara

The Column of Death

While traveling around Oaxaca, be sure to stop by the Zapotec archaeological area known as Mitla and give a big hug to the Column of Death. But only if you're prepared for some potentially bad news. It's said that when someone wraps their arms around it and feels the structure move, it means that the Reaper is coming for you soon.

when he suddenly discovered he had an extra mule in his train. This mule happened to be carrying an unusually large box—so heavy that it caused the mule to collapse and die. Inside was a statue of Our Lady of Solitude. Instead of putting it on trial for mule murder, the people of the region took it as a sign of great portent and immediately set about building a shrine, then a church, and then a whole basilica to worship the statue. Visitors today can go to the entrance and see a boulder that marks the exact spot where the mule died. After all that, spending a night looking at a bunch of carved radishes probably won't seem strange in the slightest.

BATTLE OF THE ORANGES

Total Citric Conflict

ITALY

Who doesn't love an orange? A magnificent fruit that provides humankind with a delicious food, juice, and the perfect mixer for alcoholic beverages. Plus, if you think a little outside the box, you'll also find they make excellent projectile weapons.

Every year in the Alpine town of Ivrea, in the northern section of Italy, the residents put on a carnival during which they pelt one another with breakfast's favorite fruit. *La Battaglia delle Arance* isn't some chaotic, willy-nilly food fight either. Nine organized teams dressed in Renaissance garb (and colored T-shirts so you can tell who's who) wage tactical battles over three days in early February. You can choose to root for:

- Chessmen
- Arduini
- Ace of Spades
- Death
- Tuchini
- Devils
- Mercenaries
- Panthers
- Credenari

Cheer as the combatants deploy their vitamin C–rich ordnance (a low-quality orange imported from Sicily) in their campaign toward total, incredibly messy victory.

How did such a custom originate? Was it some sort of localized demonstration in protest of the ravages of scurvy? Well, there's no definitive explanation in the history books, but the most popular story says it's a commemoration of the area's rebellion against a thirteenth-century tyrannical marquis who tried to force himself on a young commoner (the old practice of *jus primae noctis*, where nobility used to invite themselves along on honeymoons). But instead of falling victim to his attacks, the girl cut his royal head clean off, igniting the rage of the townsfolk and inspiring them to storm the castle. Originally the people threw beans and confetti at each other to celebrate what must have been a very bloody night, and eventually the ammunition evolved to become oranges. So why that fruit and not some other early-morning fare like grapefruit? It's said that at some point in the 1800s, young women would throw oranges down at the young men riding in carriages during parades in

Um, I Guess I'll Have the Haggis Instead

To keep up your strength during the conflict, *sanguinaccio dolce* is a popular carnival food. Traditionally consumed immediately prior to Ash Wednesday, it's prepared by mixing still–warm pig's blood with chocolate and cream to make a pudding that's both salty and sweet. A favorite treat of Hannibal Lecter (according to his TV series), it can be fashioned into a festive log or simply use it as a dip for cookies or for the random body parts of your victims. Dig in!

Hands Off, Fruit-Toucher

Fruit procurement is a little different at food stalls in Italy as compared to American supermarkets. If you visit a vendor it's considered the height of rudeness to fondle the merchandise, for example. It's also a major faux pas to tell the merchant which fruit you'd like to be placed in your bag, as it implies he or she is ignorant of their trade. If you wind up with a rotten rutabaga instead of a fresh peach, maybe you should have done your homework and learned a few words of Italian on the trip over.

order to attract their attention, whereupon the young men returned fire and voilà: A tradition was born.

The battle isn't complete anarchy. No, there are rules, many of which came about in the aftermath of World War II. Before then the battles could get seriously out of hand, turn into violent disputes, and require the local cops to jump in. Now the combat is limited to specific town squares. Skirmishes are between one team that rides in carriages (representing the nefarious palace guards) and the other that includes people walking alongside the carriages to represent the rebellious townsfolk. Unless you want to spend the remainder of the week picking pulp out of your hair, you're better off on foot since the carriage riders are critically outnumbered.

Foreigners are welcome to take part in the belligerent jubilee for about $9 a ticket, but don't expect to walk away from the largest food fight in all of Italy unscathed. At the 2016 event seventy people were injured (and citric acid in the wounds *really* stings!). Not to mention the dozens stupefied by mulled wine and nauseated by the slurry of squashed oranges and horse manure. So perhaps if you're a little on the squeamish side, you should just buy the video game called "Orange Battle." Yes, someone actually developed this. It lets you enjoy *La Battaglia delle Arance* from the comfort of your couch.

LA TOMATINA

Now If We Could Just Get a Few People to Start
Throwing Cilantro

SPAIN

While tomatoes are widely feared by those in the live entertainment profession, we usually associate these vegetables (or fruits, depending how annoying you are at parties) with their contributions toward spaghetti, salsa, and BLTs. Yet in Spain, just as in Italy, the citizenry has learned to weaponize their food—and turn it into a citywide party.

La Tomatina is an annual festival that takes place on the last Wednesday of August in the eastern town of Buñol, about twenty miles from the Mediterranean Sea. There are no deeper meanings or weighty commemorations behind the event—it's just for people to have fun and let out a little aggression.

As with many ceaseless and pointless wars, nobody really knows how *La Tomatina* got started (we have always been at war with East Ragu?). But of course there are some entertaining stories. Some say it was a group of friends having a good-natured produce squabble. Others claim it's a relic of the time disgruntled townsfolk used tomatoes to attack city councilmen. Perhaps the most popular idea is that during a 1945 parade that included giant "big head" figures in the procession, some young people got a little too rowdy and caused someone's giant fake head to fall off. Enraged, the participant

🌐 Spain versus PETA

At least it's just plants and not animals getting abused during this particular festival. That can't be said for a variety of other celebrations that take place throughout Spain. Sure, you may have heard of the running of the bulls in Pamplona. But did you know about the event that centers around guillotining a goose? (We'll talk about that one later, by the way.) Or the one that celebrates the life of a saint by throwing a live goat from the top of a church? While you might be a little concerned about the waste of good food at *La Tomatina*, at least, if you attend, you won't be incurring the wrath of animal lovers everywhere.

started flailing the head around and knocked over a market stall filled with tomatoes. This prompted the crowd to invoke the five-second rule, arm themselves with vegetables, and initiate a widespread ruckus. The following year people brought their own tomatoes, and history was made.

La Tomatina seems like an innocent enough sort of jubilee (despite being messy), but it was banned for a period after the dictator Francisco Franco deemed it unworthy, reportedly because of a lack of religious significance. The people risked arrest to celebrate the festival anyway, and it was brought back in 1957, after the people held a "tomato burial," staging a mock funeral complete with musicians playing dirges and a coffin with a giant tomato inside.

After Franco died in 1975, the celebration faced no serious opposition from grumpy tyrants and has been growing in popularity ever since. Perhaps too much, in fact, as measures have had to be taken to reduce the swarm of participants and prevent things from becoming too unruly. Up until 2013, one might see as many as forty thousand to fifty thousand brave produce warriors taking part in the melee. But city administrators started worrying about the conflict getting too out of hand, so today it's limited to just twenty thousand official ticket-holding combatants. Which must come as a small relief to the local shopkeepers, who have to coat their businesses in plastic tarps to protect their property from the pulpy carnage.

La Tomatina was actually a relatively obscure event until a broadcaster named Javier Basilio spread the word of the festival throughout Spain. It became popular enough to be declared a "Festivity of International Tourist Interest" by the Secretary Department of Tourism. Some other countries were so impressed by La Tomatina that they decided to organize their own versions. Today there are similar festivals in the United States, South America, and China. They tried to get it going in India too, but the idea was scrapped on the grounds that it was a reckless waste of tomatoes. But no matter where

Tomato Oppression

All sorts of things were banned under Generalissimo Franco. After declaring that Catholicism was the only acceptable religion, he outlawed the speaking of the minority Basque and Catalan languages, any and all labor unions, and even baby names that didn't meet with his approval. To enforce his rule, as every good dictator tends to do, he formed a vast army of secret police to oppress the populace. We're not sure the La Tomatina festival includes Franco dunk tanks and/or effigies of him strategically placed as optional projectile targets for the tomatoes, but maybe that should be a thing.

else a pretender may arise, for true vegetable warfare enthusiasts the one true home of *La Tomatina* remains the small town of Buñol.

You might be curious as to how they organize this thing. Obviously they don't tip over the carts of angry street vendors anymore; that would be cruel. Today trucks ship the ammunition in from the neighboring town of Extremadura (where tomatoes are cheaper and possibly more extreme?) and deposit it in the city center, the Plaza del Pueblo. To initiate the maelstrom, one intrepid participant must succeed in climbing to the top of a greased pole and claim ownership of a prized ham that's perched at the top. This in turn leads to the firing of water cannons and signifies the official start to the battle. As for the rules? It's every man, woman, and tomato for themselves.

THE COOPER'S HILL CHEESE-ROLLING AND WAKE

The Dangers of Dairy

ENGLAND

England may not exactly be known for its fine cuisine (unless you're a connoisseur of boiled meats), but they do know their way around a wheel of cheese. Likewise, the British may not be famous for extreme sports. But...they do know their way around a wheel of cheese. So maybe it makes sense that adventurous athletes in the land of Big Ben and boring period dramas would devise a sporting competition where participants risk life and limb rolling wheels of cheese down a hill. Or maybe it's just silly. You be the judge.

Every year in Brockworth, England, the Cooper's Hill Cheese-Rolling and Wake competition pits brave sportsmen against one another amid the age-old struggle between dairy products and gravity. Although the "Wake" portion of the event thankfully does not refer to a moment of silence in remembrance of those who've perished violently in past events, that's not to say the sport is safe. But we'll get to that later. First let's talk about how it all started.

It turns out there are two plausible origin stories.

1. The first is that it was a strange way of determining cattle grazing rights back in the fifteenth century. Farmers had to take part in the competition if they wanted to get their cows fed.
2. The second holds that the tradition began as a ritual in which people would roll bundles of burning wood down a hill to kick off the new year.

Whatever the case, the contest somehow became entirely cheese-related (except for the part where they scatter pastries throughout the area to "encourage a fruitful harvest").

The rules are pretty simple: First, roll a circular, seven- to nine-pound double Gloucester cheese down a steep hill. After the master of ceremonies announces to the participants, "One to be ready, two to be steady, three to prepare, and four to be off!" glory seekers launch themselves down the hill in an

Asinine Athletics

The English really distinguish themselves in the field of goofy yet physically precarious sports, and we're not talking about cricket. From bog snorkeling to chess boxing, there's something for every level of inebriation. But being properly drunk is practically a requirement for another uniquely British sport: ferret legging. Which is precisely what it sounds like—stuffing an angry rodent down your pants and seeing how long you can take it.

Fairway Fatalities

Golf is a sport that most people associate with Great Britain, but statistics show it's not the placid, danger-free pastime one might suppose. In fact, it's reportedly more dangerous than rugby or even boxing, with more than forty thousand duffers visiting emergency rooms for a wide range of injuries—everything from joint and back pain to cranial contusions from flying balls.

attempt to be the first one to catch their cheese and cartwheel themselves to glory (or the intensive care unit).

Nowadays there are three races held each season for men and one for women. As many as forty people used to be involved in each downhill tumble, but it's been limited to just fifteen in recent years because the local ambulance service complained that they lacked the resources to treat all the casualties. The all-time champion is a man named Chris Anderson. But although he somehow managed to win twenty-two times over the years, neither a Nike sponsorship nor a Wheaties box appearance, sadly, have been forthcoming.

As for the cheese itself, it's a local hard variety (described by Cheese.com as "smooth and buttery in texture, rich and nutty yet mellow") with a wooden wrapping. Since 1988, the same woman, Diana Smart, made it especially for the competition, using traditional methods. Until 2013, that is, when the "heavy-handed" authorities threatened that she'd be held responsible for any injuries incurred that year. Thus, the past few years have seen the cheese replaced by a lightweight foam. You have to wonder if they'll make an entire hill out of the same material (maybe by piling together surplus giant "We're #1" fingers?) seeing as that's what's most responsible for all the breaks and bruises. The authorities have since distanced themselves from the festivities, presumably because involvement in blood sport is bad for reelection campaigns, and the contest is currently free from official management.

Speaking of injuries, they are regularly both plentiful and serious, as you'd imagine when you're dealing with a sport that involves hurtling bodies down uneven slopes chasing pressed curds. In addition to the overworked ambulance service mentioned earlier, local rugby players are pressed into service to act as "catchers" for the tumbling cheese chasers. Bodily trauma is practically a guarantee after each race, and a group of volunteers called Search and Rescue Aid in Disaster is on hand to help deal with the broken and bloodied. The 2018 event showed that falling arse over teakettle in the name of sport is becoming no safer with the passage of time. Champion Chris Anderson broke the all-time wins record and tore his calf muscle at the same time. Nobody died, luckily, but there was no shortage of customers for the on-site medical professionals.

So if you're up to the challenge (and have confidence in your current insurance plan), maybe you'd like to pay a visit to the southwest of England and test your mettle (along with your bone density) by chasing coagulated milk. Or you could just stop by the Cheese Rollers Inn in the nearby village of Shurdington, grab a T-shirt, and say you did. Maybe have a friend smack you with a cricket bat in the chest, legs, arms, and head a bunch of times so your story seems more credible.

THE GIANT EASTER OMELET OF BESSIÈRES

You Can't Make an Omelet Without Breaking a Few (Thousand) Eggs

FRANCE

There is no shortage of food-related traditions in France, the home of croissants, fine wine, and snail eating. There's even a frog leg–eating festival— although the rest of the world has pretty much recoiled in horror from this culinary delicacy. Still, there's lot of stuff for foodies to celebrate. The *Fête de la Truffe* (Truffle Festival) in Sarlat-la-Canéda and the *Salon du Chocolat* (Chocolate Fair) in Paris are but two events that attract foodies from far and wide. But one of the biggest happens on Easter in the southwestern town of Bessières. It's not cosmopolitan or chic. It seems more like something you might see as a promotion for the grand opening of a greasy diner in the American South (which might explain why the town of Abbeville, Louisiana, has their own version): an omelet the size of a minivan.

To prepare this absurd feast requires the sacrifice of fifteen thousand eggs and an unknown number of exhausted chickens. According to legend, this custom originated when Napoleon Bonaparte stopped by the village in between conquering Europe and enjoyed an omelet so delectable that he appropriated every egg in town in order to create a meal humongous enough to feed all his soldiers.

Garçon, There's a Gonad in My Soup

Did you think masticating on oysters and nibbling on frog legs were the grossest things the French do at their tiny café tables? Well, maybe they are if you don't mind the horse meat options you can commonly find on the menu. Or the delicious–sounding *ris de veau*, which is a nice way of saying "calf pancreas." Perhaps you'd prefer the elegance that is *frivolites beneventines couilles de mouton*, an expensive delicacy from the Périgord region, the main ingredient of which is sweet, tender sheep testicles.

Remember how we mentioned that a town in Louisiana does something similar every year? Well, they're not the only non-French locality with a strongly Gallic heritage to create their own monument to fried chicken fetuses. The official Giant Omelet Festival takes place in seven locations around the world, including multiple locations in France; Granby in Quebec, Canada; Dumbéa in the South Pacific territory of New Caledonia; Malmedy, Belgium; and Pique, Argentina. And if the city administrators of Egg, Austria, haven't yet considered applying for membership, they're really missing out on a tourism opportunity.

It's not mere amateurs who are charged with the cooking duties, by the way. Only members of the eminent Brotherhood of the Omelet (duly appointed by the Knights of the Giant Omelet) are given the weighty responsibility of cracking all the eggs and sizzling up a breakfast fit for Godzilla. The preparation involves a ridiculously large pan, of course, along with an equally immense fire and vigorous stirring with oar-sized spoons. The Brotherhood doesn't get to hog the final product all for themselves: Reasonable portions are handed out to the thousands of nonvegans in attendance.

The outsized omelet cooking is but one of the events that take place during this festival (which actually doesn't always fall on Easter, should you be hankering for a slice and don't want to show up late). Attendees can also enjoy music, dancing, parades, and the like, but you can experience that sort of stuff anywhere. The real attraction is watching very serious chefs stir up an omelet big enough to appease a giant coming through town (and maybe, in the process, raise his cholesterol to heart attack levels).

Maybe we downplayed the other attractions a little too much. At least according to the 2018 schedule of events, there do seem to be plenty of other sights to divert one's attention from the behemoth breakfast preparation. On November 3, there was a Tractor Egg Cracking Competition, which sounds wasteful yet entertaining. On the following day you had to show up early to register for an intriguing attraction called the Giant Omelet Ride. The Louisiana counterpart livened things

Down Home on the Villa

Just as the making of a giant omelet has been replicated by other countries, France's Pig–Squealing Championship strikes a familiar chord. This event, held in Trie–sur–Baïse, would make any porker proud. Contestants see who can best mimic porcine noises through different stages of their life cycle. There's also the *Fête de la Dinde in Licques*, which is a parade consisting entirely of (we're going to assume highly anxious and suspicious) turkeys.

up with an egg-cracking contest and an antique car show, while the one in Belgium is perfect for daredevils as they've had a recent egg production pesticide scare. New Caledonia brings in a merry-go-round if you need to park the kids somewhere while you scarf eggs.

THE CHINCHILLA MELON FESTIVAL

I Went to the Festival and All I Got Was This Lousy Contusion

AUSTRALIA A festival celebrating melons may not sound all that exciting. But the Chinchilla Melon Festival happens in Australia, so right there you know it's going to be a little bit weirder than your run-of-the-mill food bash. Chinchilla is the name of the town in Queensland where the event takes place, and because we know you were wondering, it has nothing to do with the delightfully snuggly South American rodent. The reason this town of only around seven thousand people celebrates the glory of all things melon is because it's where the first commercially grown specimen of that vegetable (yes, it's a vegetable) was successfully produced in the nation back in the 1950s.

The thing that sets Chinchilla's festival apart from similar expositions, the kinds that merely present attendees with various dishes and send you home bloated and broke, is the creativity (and total disregard for cleanliness) on display. At this celebration you don't just eat melons; you also get the opportunity to throw them, race with them, spit their seeds (also known as pips) for distance, and even ski across their pulpy innards. It's a nice combination of face-stuffing and cardio. It also is only held once every two years, which should give you plenty of time to get your melon-shaped body in shape for the next one.

Better Bring Some Antivenom Just in Case

Gliding across a parking lot filled with melon guts isn't the only way to enjoy winter sports in Australia. There are places to visit if you don't have the urge to strap on a pair of skis. Ben Lomond, Tasmania, may not compare with Banff or Sugarloaf, but where else can you go if you want to snowboard down a frozen hill in July? And be relatively free from the threat of deadly poisonous jellyfish, snakes, spiders, crocodiles (and God knows what else) to boot?

Chinchilla has good reason to be grateful for melons (watermelons, specifically). Recognized as Australia's "melon capital," the region now grows 25 percent of all watermelons in the country, bringing prosperity to the local farmers and everyone else in the vicinity. The February festival began in 1994, when a drought was ravaging the region, and it helped the people to withstand the economic downturn when they shifted their efforts temporarily toward tourism. The sloppy fun now lasts an entire week, and attendance has grown exponentially in the decades since its beginning. People from all over the country (and the world) show up to take part in wild and crazy events.

If you're still on the fence about whether you should cancel all other plans in February in order to take part in the next Chinchilla Melon Festival, here are some of the events that we didn't mention that you'll be sad you missed out on:

- A melon chariot race, where people construct vehicles out of cardboard packing cartons and pallets, then complete a lap on a course littered with melon rinds without falling off.

- A melon ironman/woman competition, wherein hardy competitors complete grueling challenges and over-come obstacles while holding a melon (which must remain intact).
- The melon bungy, where youngsters attached to elastic ropes pull against one another on a melon-coated mat in an attempt to reach (you guessed it) a melon.

Oh, and there was also a melon rodeo, a melon chef, a melon street parade, and a melon beach party. Also a number of vendors selling all manner of melon-themed apparel. Plus an appearance by "Australia's Top Poet" Gary Fogarty. Who, we have to assume, made up a bunch of rhymes about melons.

The nearest big city to Chinchilla is Brisbane, which is just three and a half hours away by car in case you don't want to stay in a campground surrounded by the stench of rotting

Speed Humps

Now that you're good and sticky from wallowing in smashed watermelons, it's time to get nice and stinky. That shouldn't be hard to accomplish at the Uluru Camel Cup, an annual race held in the Northern Territory of Central Australia. An Outback location sacred to the Aborigines, it's also home to the world's largest number of feral camels (you'd assume they're much more eager to spit on your face than the domesticated versions). The first Uluru Camel Cup was held in 2012 on a Wednesday. Because Wednesday is Hump Day. Get it? Anyway, it was a big success and because we know you won't be able to sleep tonight without knowing, the winning camel was named Lazy Dazy.

produce. It's also within driving distance of the famed Gold Coast and just two hours away from Toowoomba (if you want to send your friends interesting postcards). There's even a small airfield available for the courageous. Charter flights are available if you're game for landing on a grass strip that may or may not be infested with aggressive marsupials.

ROADKILL COOK-OFF

Is That Opossum or Armadillo in Your Teeth?

UNITED STATES Hey, c'mon! Who doesn't love a possum that's been squashed flat as a pancake by a semi? Or a skunk that's been dead for a week? Where's your spirit of culinary adventure?

In the United States, every state has its own official cuisine the residents love to celebrate. Whether it's Texas chili, Maryland crabs, or Alaskan salmon, you can count on local festivals throughout the year where you can sample the most famous local dishes. In West Virginia, where the state fruit is the Golden Delicious apple, wouldn't you suppose their most well-known food festival revolves around apple pies? Nope. It celebrates the type of stuff that normally only a desperate vulture would find edible.

The annual West Virginia Roadkill Cook-Off, held near the Shenandoah National Park and put on by the Pocahontas County Chamber of Commerce, happens concurrently with the region's Autumn Harvest Festival in late September. But the menu at the roadkill festival is less of the agricultural variety and more what you pried from your car grill after driving through the hinterlands. But don't worry: People aren't actually cooking the corpses of desiccated woodchucks or raccoons. No, they're cooking *fresh* woodchucks and raccoons.

And opossum, squirrels, lizards...anything else that doesn't know enough to stay away from high-speed traffic.

The competition itself is between amateur chefs (so Guy Fieri won't be sneaking in to win the event with groundhog bouillabaisse) with dishes that include novel ingredients such as elk, black bear, snapping turtle—theoretically anything that moves (but isn't fast enough to avoid a pickup truck). Although the menu doesn't really include creatures that suffered death by misadventure on the highway, eating real roadkill cuisine happens to have a history in parts of West Virginia. That sort of thing was considered a smart way of using scarce resources.

As for the prizes? Each cooking team gets a hundred bucks just for signing up early, which is a pretty decent incentive. The grand prize winner gets a $1,200 check, along with an engraved cutting board. Not too shabby, unless you're one of the contestants who spend about that much on travel, tents, and ingredients (which some choose to hunt for themselves). You

🔍 Just Makes Your Mouth Water, Doesn't It?

As you're surely curious about some of the specifics regarding the scrumptious offerings available, here's a sampling from the 2018 menu at the festival:

- Hillbilly Mardi Gras Alligator & Turtle Gumbo
- Fender Fried Fawn Smothered in Vulture Vomit
- Drunken Deer in the Headlights
- Solomon A Gundy (deer and alligator)
- And the winner: Predator Prey Chili (a bear/venison combo)

can't put a price tag on pride, however, and surely any monetary compensation can hardly compare with the admiring stares from children as they gobble down your rabbit Alfredo and iguana tacos. Laugh all you want, but the grub is impressive enough to have attracted visits from the Food Network, the Travel Channel, and the Discovery Channel. Presumably it won't be long until Netflix uses the location as the setting for a horror movie about four-legged chili ghosts or something.

But the festival isn't all about chowing down on teriyaki bear meat, quail meatballs, and squirrel gravy over biscuits. There's also live Appalachian mountain music, a 5k "Possum Trot" walk/run, a variety of vendor booths, and a bounce house for the kids. You can even root for your favorite senior citizen in the Ms. Grandma Roadkill Pageant.

The whole thing is treated in a tongue-in-cheek manner, but it provides some serious revenue for the cash-strapped region, drawing curious (and brave) visitors from around the country. It's all just a fun way of embracing the sorts of unflattering stereotypes about rural Southerners and a smart way for the citizens of one of America's poorest states to invigorate the economy. As one local resident describes it, "It's a stab at what other Americans think of us West Virginians. They call us rednecks, but that can be a compliment down here. This is about having fun. It's about economic rejuvenation." In the gastrointestinal sense, however, one has to imagine it's still a bit of a struggle.

NATURE

THE KARNI MATA TEMPLE

INDIA The nation of India is a land of countless amazing and beautiful temples. From the majesty of the Taj Mahal to the smaller holy sites that dot both the countryside and urban areas, there's a place to suit just about everyone's worshipping needs. Even those who pray to rats. That's right. We said rats.

The Karni Mata Temple in the small town of Deshnoke, within the northern state of Rajasthan, also goes by the charming name "The Rat Temple." And no, that's not a euphemism for a place where talkative mobsters go to pray after they squeal to the feds. Making the temple dedicated to Hanuman, the Hindu monkey god, look downright sanitary, Karni Mata is home to 25,000 black rats (which are referred to as *kabbas*, meaning "little children"). Contrary to common sense, it draws thousands of devout and curious visitors from not just India but around the world. You're welcome to feed treats to the holy rodents, just so long as you don't mind a little ankle nibbling. When that does inevitably occur, do your utmost to keep any stomping impulses in check, as any dead *Rattus rattus* must be replaced with a rat statue made out of solid silver.

How did this house of rodential reverence come to be? As legend has it, the individual for whom the temple was named,

A Golden Rat

You can also replace a rat you inadvertently squished with a replica made out of gold. How much will that run you? Well, the average adult black rat, not taking into account how fat the ones at the temple must be, weighs around twelve ounces. And let's say the current price of gold, which can fluctuate, is $1,300 per ounce. That would total up to $15,600. Our advice: Wear moccasins or some sort of bunny slippers before entering.

Karni Mata, was a woman who lived during the fourteenth century. She ordered Yama, the God of Death, to resurrect her son after he died in a drowning accident. Yama claimed that he was unable to do so, but that Karni Mata herself could do so because she was an incarnation of Durga, a principal Hindu goddess. So she did, and as a bonus made things so that her family members would all be reincarnated as rats and could no longer die. Whether that's a fair trade-off or not depends on your tolerance for pestilence and hairless tails. And why she didn't choose an animal a bit more aesthetically pleasing, like, say, a toad, is a mystery for the ages. To this day somewhere around six hundred families in the area claim to be descendants of Karni Mata and look forward to an eternity of scritching and scurrying.

Interspersed among the multitudes of black rats are a very few white ones. They're considered to be extra-holy, and if you see one you get a special blessing. So to encourage them to make an appearance visitors put out a sweet, holy food called prasad. A can of pressurized processed cheese spread may be a cheaper option but would admittedly be less holy.

Maharaja Mouthful

Singh's full title is, get ready for it...General His Highness Maharajadhiraj Raj-Rajeshwar Narendra Shiromani Maharaja Sir Ganga Singh Bahadur, Maharaja of Bikaner, GCSI, GCIE, GCVO, GBE, KCB. But you can call him "Big G" for short. What's he going to do about it? He's dead.

You'll have to get up bright and early to be the first in, as doors open at 4:00 a.m. But once inside, you'll be able to witness priests offering the rats a special worship food called *bhog* and show your appreciation by donating *dwar-bhent* to the religious staff and workers, or *kalash-bhent* for maintenance and development costs. Or you could just cut out the middleman and pelt the rats with rupees when they get too close. Actually, you probably shouldn't do that.

The man responsible for bringing forth this monument to bewhiskered plague-carriers was General Maharaja Sir Ganga Singh (1880–1943), who is remembered as a reformer and visionary. In addition to founding colleges for women, introducing modern railroads and electric grids, and introducing prison reforms, he also successfully managed a terrible famine that occurred in the state of Bikaner. Perhaps it was the prison and the famine that led to his love affair with the lowly rat? Whatever the reason, he commissioned the creation of the temple's beautiful marble architecture and donated the stately silver doors, emblazoned with images of rat-related legends, at the entrance to the inner sanctum.

Today the best time to visit the Karni Mata Temple and have a rat run across your feet (which is considered very auspicious indeed) is during two annual festivals. The first fair is the bigger one and is held somewhere between the months of March and April during the "*Navratras* from *Chaitra Shukla Ekam* to *Chaitra Shukla Dashmi*." The second fair happens between September and October, also during the *Navratras*, from "*Ashvin Shukla* to *Ashwin Shukla Dashmi*." If you'd like to look up what all that means, you can find an article on *Travelers Today* that describes the whole thing. At any rate, once there, you can follow in the footsteps of the devotees to the rodent goddess and also the contestants in an exceptionally verminous season of the reality show *The Amazing Race*. Oh, and Morgan Spurlock was also there in 2016 to film a documentary called *Rats*. Which makes a whole lot of sense. But unless you suffer from a severe case of musophobia (fear of rats and mice), the fear of hideous rodent-borne pathogens shouldn't deter you from stopping by for a look. Believe it or not, there's no recorded case of anyone ever getting the plague from being in close contact with the rats. Plus, there's likely a whole lot less poop in the air than at the temple for that monkey god.

DAY OF THE GOOSE

With all the annual festivals centered on either harassing animals, placing them in danger, or outright murdering them, Spain is a pretty terrible place to be a farm animal. Not that it's exactly a picnic for domesticated critters anywhere else, since they're often the main course, but Spain stands out in its efforts to make the lives of livestock as unpleasant as possible. But if you thought forcing confused bulls to chase tourists down the street or tossing terrified goats out of church towers was the worst of it, you haven't seen what the poor geese have to endure year after year: a yearly celebration that revolves entirely around snapping their necks for sport. Welcome to the *Día de los Gansos*, or the Day of the Goose.

The "sport" known as goose pulling was a popular pastime in various areas all around Europe during the Middle Ages (and even enjoyed a brief resurgence in the American South before the late 1700s). But today the Spanish town of Lekeitio, located on the Bay of Biscay in Basque Country, is one of the few places where it continues to flourish. The rules of the activity are simple: Every September 5, a (mercifully) deceased and oiled-up goose is tied to a rope that's strung across a stretch of water. Participants then take a flying leap in an attempt to grab the goose, decapitate it, and thus scar the psyches of any children in attendance. To make the task more difficult and entertaining, men on each end of the rope pull on it violently once a participant gets a firm handhold on the goose. This causes the man or woman doing the grabbing to fly into the air, up to six stories. The goose is dismembered in a way that PETA would probably consider a war crime.

Another variation on the goose-throttling theme takes place in the village of El Carpio de Tajo in the Spanish province of Toledo. Here it's horses that are part of the event, but thankfully they aren't beheaded before cheering crowds. In this version the goose, again, lucky to be dead, is strung up in

Saintly Goat Tossing

We mentioned goat tossing earlier, and since you may be curious as to what in the world we were talking about, here you go. In honor of St. Vincent, every June, the small village of Manganeses de la Polvorosa hurls a live goat from the highest point of the local church. Thankfully, there are folks on the ground who catch the goat with a sheet, but this does little to placate the animal activists who see no point in scaring the bejeezus out of an innocent goat. No one can even say for sure why this custom began, although our favorite legend says that in the 1700s, an intrepid goat snuck into a church to steal the food a priest had left out for the birds. When the priest found the goat the animal panicked, made a run for it, and jumped from the belfry, making a miraculous four-hoofed landing. Whereupon it scampered into the woods, leaving behind onlookers who found the incident impressive enough to link it to a saint.

the middle of a street down which riders charge while attempting to seize the bird's neck. The outcome is pretty much the same—a headless waterfowl showering its bodily contents all over the area. The point of it all is to celebrate the people's liberation from Arab control in 1141 and has been held every July on the feast day of Santiago, the patron saint of Spain, for the past 400 years. Making this possibly the darkest day for geese everywhere since the invention of the airplane propeller.

We don't mean to pick on Spain too much here, as there are other European nations that still practice similar traditions:

- Belgium
- The Netherlands
- Germany
- Switzerland
- France
- Italy

Lekeitio may be the only place where they add the aquatic aspect into the mix, but Italy changes things up by mutilating turkeys, while France includes rabbits in the decapitation

The Pero Palo Festival

Donkeys are another species of unfortunate beasts that are regularly tormented during celebrations. The Pero Palo Festival is held in the Spanish town of Villanueva de la Vera each year and is meant to commemorate the capture of a notorious sex offender. So it makes perfect sense that part of the event includes getting a donkey drunk and forcing it to haul the town's heaviest man (also drunk, naturally) through the streets while screaming crowds (yes, drunk as well) fire shotguns and bang on drums next to the animal's ears. Hold on; upon closer scrutiny, that doesn't appear to make much sense at all. Unless the sex offender was some sort of were-donkey, in which case all this is quite fitting and proper.

jubilee. Treating animals in this manner used to be part of a harvest sacrifice custom, it's believed, but nowadays it just seems like a fun thing to do during Carnival season. At least these creatures are in no danger of going extinct. But don't expect any geese, rabbits, or turkeys to go out their way to help you change a tire on the side of the road anytime soon.

As blood sports go, goose pulling may not be as bad as many other festivals around the world that put animal abuse center stage. At least the birds are dead, which wasn't always the case (when Spain came up with the concept in the 1100s the geese were very much alive and honking). During the brutal dictatorship of Francisco Franco between 1936 and 1975, an animal protection law put a stop to the bloody custom. But when Spain gained its freedom after the despot's death, it was back to every goose for himself. So if you ever run across a goose that's a raging fascist, you'll understand its point of view a little better.

FERRET LEGGING

A Pantful of Pain

GREAT BRITAIN It may come as a surprise to many, but Great Britain is home to a great many reckless and inexplicably silly customs. After all, its citizens are the ones (as we mentioned elsewhere in the book) who popularized the idea of bungee jumping. But as seemingly pointless as "sports" like shin kicking and chasing cheese wheels down a rugged slope might be, inarguably the most inscrutable decision the English ever made, at least since prime minister Neville Chamberlain made Hitler pinkie swear not to be mean, has to be "ferret legging." Which is exactly what it sounds like: stuffing rage-filled, toothy predators down a man's trousers and seeing how long he can take his delicates being mauled by a polecat.

To provide more detail on how one is declared the victor in this epic struggle of man's inner thighs versus rodent, we must find someone who's actually willing to take part in the competition. This can be problematic, mostly because one of the rules is that all participants must be completely sober. The men who choose to compete are also prohibited from wearing any underwear. But we're getting ahead of ourselves a bit.

Once the two dauntless athletes are prepared both mentally and physically, two live ferrets are shoved down their pants

Beware the Purring of the Cornish Coal Miners

Surely you're now curious as to what "shin kicking" entails, so we'll be happy to elaborate. This pastime, which may also be referred to (much less descriptively) as "hacking" or "purring," got its start way back in the early 1600s among Cornish miners who presumably lacked excitement in their lives. The rules are as follows: Two combatants face off against one another, each grabbing the other's shirt collar. They then proceed to slam their boot-clad feet against each other's tibia until one of them decides he's had enough pain for the day and cries, "Sufficient!" Overseeing the match is a referee, called a "stickler," who makes sure the event proceeds according to proper protocols. Of which there are apparently few, as the wearing of steel-toed boots used to be considered fair play.

while the tops and bottoms are tied off with rope. As entering a declawed ferret into the competition is presumably grounds for disqualification, spectators are assured that a maximum amount of flesh rending and desecration of tender bits will occur.

Many might believe that it wouldn't take more than a few seconds of incurring multiple thigh lacerations to bring each match to a rapid close. Yet the world record holder for ferret legging, a miner from Yorkshire named Reg Mellor, was able to endure the rampaging varmints in his pants for five hours and twenty-six minutes. He described the biggest obstacle he had to overcome to achieve his status as King of the Ferret Leggers, in painful detail, in an interview with Outside Online. "The ferrets must have a full mouth o' teeth. No filing of the teeth; no clipping. No dope for you or the ferrets. You must be sober, and the ferrets must be hungry—though any ferret'll eat yer eyes out even if he isn't hungry."

🔍 Evil Shark Piranhas with Fur-Coated Feet

Ferrets, while small, fuzzy, and cute, are natural-born killers despite being popular as pets. With nicknames like "shark of the land," "piranhas with feet," and "fur-coated evil," they are vicious meat eaters that must constantly murder prey in order to account for their rapid metabolism. Wild ones will greedily devour every part of their victims, right down to the bones, skin, feathers, and fur. Ferrets are not generally harmful to humans, however, unless they're inspired to exact bloody vengeance on any nearby genitals after being placed in a tied-up pair of pants.

It's said that ferret legging began for one of two possible reasons:

1. Back when poachers used the small mammals to root out smaller prey on other people's land, they often hid them down their pants to avoid appearing suspicious.
2. Legitimate hunters did the same thing, except the purpose was to keep the ferrets warm when the weather was chilly.

We have to assume that even back then in the days of the sport's origins, the people involved had their undercarriages protected by some sort of thick undergarment. Which makes it all the more puzzling why modern ferret-legging enthusiasts would agree to do without any sort of barrier. And if you're wondering if they really do see that portion of the male anatomy as something that's worthy of sinking their teeth into, let's have our friend Reg Mellor clarify the situation again: "Do they! Why, I had 'em hangin' from me tool for hours an' hours an' hours! Two at a time—one on each side."

While there was once an effort to include women in the sport, by putting ferrets down their blouses and calling it "ferret busting," it sadly failed to catch on. Even more regrettably, despite the fact that ferret legging has existed for hundreds of years and enjoyed a brief resurgence in the 1970s, it's considered a dying sport today. Perhaps this is for the best, for the welfare of the ferrets if nothing else. After all, in normal circumstances a domesticated ferret can be a loving, sweet-natured household pet. But at their worst, for instance when forced into a man's pants, they can be as our expert Reg Mellor explains, "cannibals, things that live only to kill, that'll eat your eyes out to get at your brain." If the inimitable Mr. Mellor has not yet been elevated to take his place among the pantheon of great English poets, please join us in formally recommending him.

THE CALAVERAS COUNTY FROG JUMPING JUBILEE

A Hopping Good Time

UNITED STATES Those familiar with the works of Mark Twain (or Samuel Clemens if you're fancy) will recognize his short story "The Celebrated Jumping Frog of Calaveras County" as the work that propelled him to international fame. While the plot of the story may not be entirely rooted in fact, the actual county of Calaveras, California, does exist. It also hosts a frog-based athletic exhibition every third weekend in May. While making ill-advised bets on the outcome, like the character in Twain's tale, is a private decision, anyone can stop by to watch as children and adults alike violently slap the ground to make frogs leap in terror and get across the finish line first.

The Jumping Frog Jubilee has been a staple at the Calaveras County Fairgrounds in the city of Angels Camp since 1928 (when it was organized to celebrate the paving of the town's main road), allowing anyone with the will and a frog to compete for a cash prize. Tragically, seven-time title winner Bill Proctor passed away in 2018, but before he went on to the great lily pad in the sky, he was an inspiration to countless wranglers of slimy contenders. He was even there when the world-record jump occurred, as he recalled in an interview with ABC10 News out of Sacramento: "The world record is twenty-one feet, five and three-quarter inches. That record was set in 1986 by a frog named 'Rosie the Ribiter.'"

If you win the hopping contest, you get your name emblazoned upon an impressive brass plaque, which will then be mounted in a place of honor on a sidewalk in Angels Camp's downtown area. This historic section of the town is known reverentially as the Frog Hop of Fame. Victors are awarded a $900 prize. And should some young upstart somehow break the long-standing record of Rosie the Ribiter, that will net them a cool $5,000. The winning frog unfortunately has no legal claim to the prize money in the state of California, as far as we're aware. But chances are it would waste the cash on gourmet flies and other such frivolousness.

There are other frog-jumping contests across the continental United States, from alternate sites in California to various towns in Ohio, all the way up to Piscataquis County, Maine. Canada has its own version called the St. Pierre Frog Follies in Manitoba. But Angels Camp in Calaveras County will always be the original, and is unlikely to be forgotten unless the works

Ostrich Racing Is a Thing Too

If watching frogs hop their way to victory doesn't tickle your fancy, perhaps you'd rather watch giant flightless birds compete instead. At Southern California's annual Riverside County Fair & National Date Festival, ostrich races have been a tradition for years, as has the equally entertaining sport of camel racing. Ostriches can reach speeds of up to 45 mph, which is pretty impressive for something so ridiculous-looking. They have jockeys atop them as well, so any high-speed crashes and multibird collisions are bound to be much more entertaining than anything at a NASCAR event.

of Mark Twain somehow get forgotten too. It's also a wonderful diversion for the citizens of an area that has a pretty dark history. *Calaveras* is the Spanish word for "skulls," an ominous but fitting name for a place that had the highest number of recorded suicide deaths in the United States in 2015. Calaveras County earned its macabre title when a Spanish explorer arrived in the area and discovered a number of skulls lining the banks of a stream. It was officially given its name a couple of decades later when another band of explorers went to sleep one night and woke up to find themselves surrounded by an alarmingly large amount of human bones. So yeah, it must have come as a relief to be known for a frog-jumping contest instead.

If you're worried about the welfare of the creatures that do most of the work, you'll be happy to know that the Jumping Frog Jubilee has measures in place to prevent its web-footed

The Twentynine Palms Weed Show

If you prefer your competitions to be focused on flora instead of fauna, California has another yearly shindig held the first weekend of each November called the Twentynine Palms Weed Show. No, not *that* type of weed. Considering the state in which it's held, your confusion is understandable. No, the nonhallucinogenic sorts of weeds. At this event, located in the inhospitable low-desert region of the state, contestants compete to create the prettiest floral arrangements using indigenous plants that grow in the surrounding area, such as tumbleweeds and various cacti. The Weed Show got its start back in 1941, well before anyone would think of giggling at the name.

athletes from...croaking. There's a limit to how long a single frog can participate in the events, and the use of the endangered California red-legged frog (or any other rare amphibian) is strictly prohibited. Thanks to small efforts like these, animal lovers will be pleased to learn that this particular frog appears to be making a comeback. Needless to say, shoving lead shot down a frog's throat as happened in Twain's story is also frowned upon and likely grounds for immediate dismissal. And considering how much California is concerned with protecting animals, you'll probably be lucky not to be placed on a raft and banished into the Pacific Ocean.

THE MONKEY BUFFET FESTIVAL
Making the Best of a Monkey Invasion

THAILAND

Thailand is famous for its grand and historic Buddhist temples, which attract thousands of foreign tourists each year, who take in the architectural and cultural splendor. There are no fewer than 40,717 of them decorating the landscape, and each one is unique. Thailand's also famous for monkeys. And in one notable region, those two things come together.

No temples are stranger than the ones known as Wat Phra Sri Rattana Mahathat and Phra Prang Sam Yot, located in and near the town of Lopburi. Mostly because they're both crawling with wild monkeys. In fact, the entire town of Lopburi is. But instead of calling a primate exterminator or a team of professional monkeybusters, the residents just decided to roll with it and created a festival celebrating the fact that they've been overrun.

Lopburi is one of Thailand's oldest cities, but since it's a bit off the beaten path it probably wouldn't attract much attention if it wasn't for its annual Monkey Festival. This event, which became a tradition in 1989, attracts swarms of human visitors every late November to even further test the limits of the town's ability to accommodate interloping primates. Despite being held near those Buddhist temples we mentioned, there's nothing spiritual about the Monkey Buffet. Yes, you heard right, we said "buffet." The centerpieces of the Monkey Festival are huge towers of fruits and vegetables upon which the simians can unleash their primal savagery. But before those are rolled out, the festivities are opened with dance routines performed by men wearing monkey costumes. The man who came up with the idea of the town hosting a yearly macaque food orgy, Yongyuth Kitwattananusont, once even dressed up in a furry costume himself and parachuted into the middle of things to kick off the festivities. What emotions are going through the heads of the monkeys during these activities can only be guessed, although impatience is probably foremost.

Monkeys do enjoy a certain amount of respect throughout Thailand, thanks to the two-thousand-year-old legend of Prince Rama, who found himself in the position of having to save his wife, Princess Sita, from the clutches of a demon lord named

The Surin Elephant Roundup

The northeast province of Surin is where Thailand celebrates a much larger animal, the elephant. Their traditional roundup of this beast, which the Thai people consider royal, is also held each November and includes a spectacular parade that stars two hundred elephants dressed up in full decorative regalia. Surin is considered the best place for this event, as the area is famous for raising and taming the mighty pachyderm. But the people appear to be kind to their massive charges. One of the most important parts of the festival is when the parade ends, at which time tourists get to watch as the elephants enjoy a hearty breakfast.

Ravana. Lucky for him Hanuman, the monkey god, entered the picture, and with the help of his new ally's primate army, Rama was able to win the day. Subsequently, according to the story, Rama returned home to rule the land for the next ten thousand years. Which...didn't appear to pan out, unless he, that monkey god, and his entire kingdom are really great at hiding.

At any rate, back to the Monkey Festival. In advance of the event, while food preparers are assembling the mountains of produce, invitations are handed out to the monkeys in the form of cashew nuts with a note wrapped around them. However, it's likely that this step is wholly unnecessary, as it's widely known that macaques don't adhere to social niceties. Indeed, while tourists are in abundance and expected to be on their best behavior, the monkeys can do whatever they damn well want. As wild simians are generally wont to do, they are prone to throwing the food (and God knows what else) around, basically creating havoc and making themselves an affront to polite

Coconut-Picking Macaques

The type of monkey that infests Lopburi, the macaque (say it ten times fast and see how long it takes to get thrown out of a Starbucks), isn't just known for invading small towns and freeloading meals. Innovative Thai farmers have given these monkeys gainful employment, sending them up trees on a leash to pick coconuts. There's even a Monkey Training School in the city of Surat Thani, where young macaques can make their parents proud by learning a trade. The founder, Somporn Saekhow, created the school as an alternative to the more abusive methods of coercing macaques to work for a living. Disdaining the use of any force or violence, he's seen his idea become a great success with the farmers. We can safely assume the monkeys appreciated it as well.

society. Wisely, human guests are not allowed to join the monkeys at the fruit and vegetable towers and are instead limited to nearby food stalls and dining areas. We're not sure if these rules have always been in place, but it's likely they have been ever since someone in local government brought up the dangers of monkey bite liability lawsuits.

For the year-round residents of Lopburi, the rampaging macaques are considered a cell phone–stealing, hair-pulling, publicly defecating menace. But they're a cross that becomes much easier to bear when all the tourist money is counted up. When hotel owner Yongyuth Kitwattananusont came up with the concept decades ago, he surely would never have guessed that it would become such a sensation. Enough to where the Tourism Authority of Thailand now sponsors the proceedings, trying to lure as many monkey-loving folks as possible from around the world. And it's surely in Lopburi's best interest to keep the festival going, no matter the cost. Because nobody wants to be around for the screeching apocalypse that will take place when a large number of entitled monkeys are denied their free annual feast.

LIVE FISH SLURPING AT THE KRAKELINGEN FESTIVAL

Bottoms Up, *Grondeling* Down

BELGIUM

Slurping down a whole, live fish is never recommended, unless it's absolutely necessary during some bizarre circumstance involving a life-or-death game of Truth or Dare or something. It's true that goldfish swallowing became a fad among college students in America during the 1930s, before there were any animal rights groups to protest. And opening your mouth and sending a wriggling sea creature down the hatch goes back a lot longer than that. The people of Belgium have been doing it for centuries, in fact, during an event they call the *Krakelingen* Festival.

The *Krakelingen* Festival takes place the last Sunday of every February and is held to celebrate the coming of spring. There are lots of activities, including a food fight in which people hurl bread rolls called *krakelingen* at one another, which is how the festival got its name. They're meant to commemorate an incident that took place in medieval times, when townsfolk who were under siege taunted their antagonists by launching bread over the walls to show they had more food than the enemy force had patience. Reportedly fish were also thrown over the walls, which may explain in part why the festival also includes the live fish gulping. The small fish, known as *grondeling*, are dipped in red wine first to calm them down a bit prior

🔍 The Cat-Throwing Festival

Every three years in the Belgian town of Ypres, they throw a bash that surely drives all cat lovers on the Internet into a frenzy of high-pitched squeals. The Cat Parade features feline-based floats aplenty along with cat-fancying revelers in furry costumes and bewhiskered face paint. At one of the stages of the parade, a man dressed in a jester's costume pushes plush cat toys off of a church belfry. Hundreds of years ago this celebration involved throwing actual cats from the seventy-foot-high platform to their doom. This ungrateful practice was meant to commemorate a good deed the town's cats performed. They got rid of the rats infesting an important civic building where the townsfolk stored their cloth goods. Years later the citizens finally figured out that all cats were not in fact in league with Satan and changed things up so that only stuffed kitties were placed at risk.

to their ordeal. So all in all it might be a kinder fate than what happens to seafood in many sushi restaurants.

In addition to flinging bread and fish, other eye-catching parts of the *Krakelingen* Festival include Celtic druids, people in devil costumes chasing people in snowman costumes, and other subjects based on folklore and whimsy. Before the biscuit chucking begins, the bakery-fresh ammunition gets a blessing in the town chapel. Local bigwigs then initiate the hostilities by winging the *krakelingen* into the crowd assembled outside. This crowd can be quite big, since one of the *krakelingen* contains an expensive piece of jewelry. There's an unruly atmosphere as adults and children scramble and squabble to acquire a €750 trinket. When night finally comes, a large stake

The Carnival of Bears

Providing more evidence that Belgians can't get enough of dressing up like animals, there's an entirely different town where inhabitants dress up in bear suits. This festival is called the Carnival of Bears and is held in Andenne. The inspiration for this citywide fete thankfully didn't come from that creepy scene in *The Shining* but rather an equally disconcerting incident long ago in which a little boy managed to kill a rampaging bear with a hammer. And it wasn't just any little boy—it was Charles Martel, the rightful sovereign of all the lands. Unlike the Cat Parade, live bears were never tossed from on top of a church, likely due to logistical reasons. Plus, it probably would have proved rather traumatizing to children in attendance, so the shrewd decision was made to throw teddy bears instead.

is set on fire in a manner reminiscent of the Celtic rituals of old, while everyone dances, sings, and slurps free soup. But as we mentioned earlier, soup isn't the only thing being slurped; for hundreds of years the traditional festivities have also included the heartless quaffing of countless scaly innocents. Which we shall refer to henceforth as The Silence of the *Grondeling*.

Predictably, animal rights defenders have taken extreme exception to the part of the festival with the fish. Not because fish shouldn't ever be a part of any menu but more because, as a former mayor of Geraardsbergen named Guido de Padt explained in an interview with *The International Herald Tribune*, "Sometimes they are still trembling a little in your mouth." Before the *krakelingen* pelting began, for ages it was customary for the local civic leaders to plop *grondelings* into a ceremonial sixteenth-century goblet so they could be sent alive down your gastrointestinal tract. Those who are outraged at

the way the *grondelings* meet their maker have been successful in convincing organizers to limit the amount of fish gulped
during the event. The ultimate goal is to replace them entirely
with marzipan replicas. The wriggling aspect will be absent
in that case, so perhaps organizers might consider filling the
marzipan with a live mouse or perhaps a kitten. Unless those
pesky animal rights people should somehow have a problem
with that.

TUNARAMA

If you've ever wanted to participate in a giant fish-heaving contest, have we got the place for you! Coming up on its sixtieth anniversary in 2020, Australia's Tunarama celebration is a tradition that happens in the late part of January (which is summertime in the Land Down Under) every year. It's four long days of fish-centric fun for everyone except those whose seafood allergies make their faces blow up like summer squashes. Tens of thousands of people show up in Port Lincoln, a city of about sixteen thousand located on a jutting southern tip of the state of South Australia, to partake in various activities that all have something to do with the titular fish. But the main and most popular event of the entire proceedings is the Championship Tuna Toss, where athletic competitors see who can throw a rotting koala carcass the farthest. Well, no. Of course they don't do that. What they actually do is throw a big dead tuna.

Both men and women are welcome to compete in the Tuna Toss. Amateurs and professionals are equally free to take part as well. Not that there's any such thing as a pro seafood shot putter; the closest is the world champion hammer thrower, Australian Sean Carlin, who competed in the 1992 Barcelona and 1996 Atlanta Olympic Games. On a side note, Carlin has since retired from the sport (both hammer throwing and fish throwing) and is currently a teacher. We'd be willing to bet that his students are much more impressed with his tuna accomplishments than anything else in his athletic background. In case you're curious, he threw the winning fish 37.23 meters in 1998. That's less than half the current record for hammer throwing, but hammers don't tend to be covered in ice, slime, and stink like the average frozen tuna corpse.

Tunarama began life as a way to lure tourists to out-of-the-way Port Lincoln, but since its inception it has become a beloved tradition that draws outsiders and locals alike. Along with the inevitable tuna-themed parade, attendees can also take part in sunny summer activities like sand castle building and the like, all while listening to live music and consuming mass quantities of fried foods. There's even a children's area called the Carnivale of the Sea, where adults dressed as

Kangaroo. It's What's for Dinner

The national animal of Australia is the red kangaroo. This makes perfect sense, as that creature is definitely one of the top three things that come to mind when you think of the country (along with koalas and the late Steve Irwin). But while few people in America would ever consider devouring a bald eagle, or citizens of the United Kingdom countenance the thought of dining on a bulldog, kangaroos are definitely on the menu for Aussies. From kangaroo stir–fry to kangaroo skewers in red wine marinade, greedily nibbling on large, hoppity marsupials is widely considered "fair dinkum." We're not exactly sure what that phrase means, but we'll assume it translates to "tastes gamey."

mermaids and pirates divert the kids while their parents sample the wares of the various beer and wine vendors.

But what everyone wants to see, of course, is the famous tuna-tossing contest. It's something that everyone who witnesses it will remember forever, especially the woman who took a flying frozen fish to the face in 1989 and wound up receiving $35,000 in compensation after a six-day stay in a local hospital. That incident wasn't the only controversy that Tunarama has had to overcome: in 2002, a bikini contest led to lewd and lascivious behavior, which in turn led to accusations that the event was demeaning toward women. Yet Tunarama endured, overcoming all obstacles and earning the admiration and affection of the community after providing a place for victims of raging 2005 bushfires to relieve tensions. Because nothing relieves tension like the possibility of head trauma inflicted by an airborne albacore.

The only real controversy today, and one that has reared its fishy head for years, is that the Tuna Toss seems to be a

Open Wide for the Witchetty Grub

The Witchetty grub, a plump, finger–sized moth larvae, has served as a natural fast food, or "bush tucker," for the Aboriginal Australians for eons. While one might assume that everyone else on the continent would consider the very idea of stuffing these wriggling horrors into their mouths abhorrent, increasingly they can be found for sale in major supermarkets. As for what happens when you actually do sink your teeth into one, opinions vary. Some people say if you eat them raw, the gooey center has the flavor of almonds. If consumed after some time sizzling and popping in a pan, its flavor is reportedly reminiscent of scrambled eggs. And unsurprisingly, there are also those who insist it tastes just like chicken.

thoughtless waste of perfectly good food. That's true also of the competition's junior version, in which youngsters who can't yet lift hefty frozen fish instead throw shrimp as far as they can in the "Prawn Toss." To alleviate concerns, a local artist named Ken Martin was commissioned in 2008 to construct a plastic tuna replica that would be thrown instead of an actual fish. Response to the change has been mixed, as one competitor explained to a reporter: "There's no big difference while you're throwing, but when I did it with the real tuna last time, it had defrosted in the heat and snapped. Yeah, so that was a bit dangerous, but you do lose the whole fun side of it being a fake fish." Fish dismemberment or the possibility of grievous injury? Perhaps it doesn't matter since both things sound like such a blast.

THE *MARI LWYD*

Getting Into the Spirit of the Season with a Horse Corpse

WALES

Every country that celebrates the yuletide season has its own weird way of expressing itself during the sacred holiday. Germans hang an ornamental pickle on their trees, and the Swedes build a giant Yule goat. In just about every culture during the season, though, there's a horse. After all, they were present (at least a donkey was) at the manger, according to Renaissance artists. Horses are especially important in Wales at this time of year. Only the most notable tradition there doesn't involve riding or the pulling of sleds. What the Welsh do is wear horse skulls like hats and go door-to-door, creeping the hell out of everybody.

The Welsh call their form of caroling *Mari Lwyd*, and it seems more appropriate as a Halloween activity than as a celebration of the birth of Christ. After decorating a horse skull with pretty ribbons, bows, baubles, and doodads, a band of singing Welsh folk approach the doors of town residents and sing in rhymes, requesting to come in. What ensues is a back-and-forth exchange called a *pwnco*; those inside the house are expected to sing something just as poetically witty (or more so) than the people outside the door. This goes on until everyone gets tired and wants a drink. It's sort of a trick-or-treat

🔍 The Day of the Wren

Another Welsh tradition that involves both Christmas and creatures is Wren Day. For this nineteenth-century tradition, alternately called Day of the Wren and Hunt the Wren Day, every Twelfth Night (the last day of the yuletide season) a fake wren is stuck on the top of a decorated pole. The pole is then paraded through town, held aloft by people called mummers (also wrenboys or strawboys), who dress up in masks and suits made out of straw. Tragically, in the past the wren wasn't fake, and the pole was more like a pitchfork. As the mummers came down the streets, begging for money in song, they would hand out (presumably bloody) feathers from the bird as good luck charms. Providing even further evidence that the Welsh have some significant confusion as to the difference between Christmas and Halloween.

situation, only instead of candy, the homeowner eventually has to open the door and hand out food and alcohol to the horse ghoul and his minions.

Like many traditions of this sort, the exact reason why people started terrorizing their neighbors with singing horse zombies remains shrouded in mystery. It is, however, pretty safe to assume that there's some very old religion in there somewhere.

With all the free food and booze being handed to the participants, the members of the *Mari Lwyd* have been known to transform from a band of merry revelers to an unruly and annoying mob. The fact that they visit pubs as much as houses doesn't help matters much. In some areas of Wales they have such a good time that they haul out the skull for New Year's Eve as well, pestering passersby on the street with their liquor-fue-led, barnyard demon shenanigans. Yet despite the complaints of heathenry and public drunkenness that have been lodged for hundreds of years, the poetry-battling livestock phantom continues to endure.

How to Make Your Own Seasonal Abomination

Should you happen to have a horse skull just lying around the house, or know how to acquire one without breaking any local laws, here are the official instructions from the website of Cardiff's swank Exchange Hotel, so that you can make your very own horrifying *Mari Lwyd*:

"A horse's skull (real or custom made)
Two large glass marbles or baubles
Fake ears
Ribbons for the mane
A white sheet to cover the carrier's body
A broomstick to support the skull above your head"

Once you have the materials, stuff the marbles/baubles into the eye sockets, use the ribbons to make a mane, and mount the skull onto the stick while ensuring the mouth can open and close. Then the person who's the designated carrier gets to wear a sheet and perform their best interpretation of a horse ghost.

The Exchange Hotel does admit that this custom is a little creepy but argues that it also serves to "bring communities together at Christmas time." Which, we assume, includes groups of children cowering in closets praying for Christmas to end before they get eaten by the monsters in the street.

DEATH

DANCING WITH THE DEAD
Back and Ready to Party

MADAGASCAR The first of the five stages of grief is denial, as it can be extremely difficult to accept the loss of a loved one. The last one is acceptance, and the people of the African nation of Madagascar appear to have found a way to merge those stages together in the creepiest way possible outside a remake of Alfred Hitchcock's *Psycho*: by digging up their dead relatives and parading them around town as if they just got back from an extended vacation.

Called *Famadihana*, or "the turning of the bones," the practice involves not just digging up corpses but also dressing the remains in fancy new clothes, spraying them with perfume, and dancing. And oh, yes, we don't mean people dance in a circle around the dear departed or something like that. The cadavers are fully involved in the process (although it's unlikely they lead).

It's a tradition that goes back hundreds of years. It's considered a sacred way of honoring your ancestors, strengthening bonds between the generations, and securing a little good luck on the side. It's a time to share the latest hot family gossip with members who've left the earthly plane and request their wise advice for the future (any actual two-way conversations that take place are probably a sign you need to see a therapist). The ritual is believed to be necessary for the spirits to gain passage to the afterlife, which only happens once total decomposition is complete. This is a process that can take many years (unless you're lucky enough to have had a relative die in a wood chipper mishap), and the dancing celebrations usually take place every five to seven years.

When Christian missionaries arrived on the scene in the seventeenth century, they were predictably horrified at *Famadihana* and did their best to shut it down. Seems a little hypocritical of a belief system that encourages believers to eat portions of their savior on Sundays, but whatever. Today, however, the Catholic Church has recognized the cultural importance of the ritual, decided it didn't infringe on their religious sovereignty, and officially "no longer objects" to the practice. The dead might even be dragged to a weekly Mass presided over by a nonplussed priest before they're returned to the family crypt. It's certainly understandable that one might find the ritual disturbing and the accompanying rites (like eating portions of the old shrouds to promote fertility) more than a little gross. But one should always keep in mind that it's all

Survival of the Weirdest

Watching people sashay around with dead relatives doesn't even register on the strange scale when you compare it to Madagascar's bizarre wildlife. After being cut off from the African mainland, evolution basically ran amok and gave the world such oddities as the world's smallest chameleon and arguably the world's most startling mammal, the aye-aye.

The Poorest Plague

In modern times, the bubonic plague has been referred to as "a disease of poverty," which is fitting since Madagascar is one of the poorest countries in the world. In addition to *Famadihana*, the reasons for its spread are the same as in medieval times: unsanitary conditions and a proximity to rats (rats are hosts to fleas, which carry the plague *Baccillus*).

about love. As one visitor to Madagascar reportedly described the experience of witnessing *Famadihana* firsthand, "I came expecting the most macabre of ceremonies but instead found an extreme form of adoration for loved ones that will forever change how I view life and death."

Not everyone is a fan of the old ways, as it can be an expensive proposition buying silk shrouds and food for the multitudes of family members who show up for the spectacle. Not to mention the expense involved in hiring musicians to play at the event and the costs to renovate a temporarily empty tomb. As one modern taxi driver, Randriamananjara Rindra, puts it, "It's a sheer waste of money. Besides, there is no relationship between the living and the dead. When you die, you're gone." But despite a drop-off in the numbers of participants, it appears that waltzing with mummified kinfolk will remain one of Madagascar's least tourist-friendly customs for the foreseeable future.

Actually, maybe not. Officials are seriously considering placing an official ban on *Famadihana*, not because of how ghastly it seems to outsiders but because it may have caused the spread of plague. You know, the one that wiped out half of Europe. Over one hundred people on the island died as a result of the Black Death in 2017. It's such an issue that surrounding nations have received an official warning from the World Health Organization to watch out when trading with Madagascar (and presumably when shaking hands with any natives who just got back after taking a few days off for a "family function"). Nonetheless there will inevitably be those who refuse to comply with any preventive measures and see such actions as a governmental conspiracy. Like the woman who stated publicly how she "will always practice the turning of the bones of my ancestors—plague or no plague. The plague is a lie." Whether she also denies the existence of measles, dysentery, and/or psoriasis is an open question.

Hopefully a compromise can be reached that satisfies all parties involved. With all the advances in special effects technology over the last few years, maybe the government could just hire some of the professionals who worked on *The Walking Dead* to make a realistic facsimile of Grandma for dancing purposes, while the real, disease-infested one remains entombed. Win-win, right?

FANTASY COFFINS

Going Out As Stylishly As Possible

GHANA

Not every culture on Earth treats the end of life with solemnity. Instead of colorless cemeteries filled with stone and sadness, there are many places (like Mexico) where the final resting places of the dearly departed are flowery and festive. In the West African nation of Ghana, they extend this idea to making the journey to the hereafter a colorful and imaginative affair. They don't so much think outside the box as much as reimagine the idea of what a box could be before it's buried in the ground.

The Ga people, an ethnic group who live in the southeastern part of the country, don't like the idea of placing their dead into boring hexagonal caskets. Instead, they insta-fashion "fantasy coffins," which are carved into shapes that reflect who and what you were before you died. For instance, if you were a fisherman, you might be interred inside a giant wooden tilapia. Or if you were a pilot, you might be fitted for a miniature airplane. If you think we're joking about a gynecologist getting buried in a massive uterus, there are pictures to prove it actually happened. At least it's a bit more complimentary than entering the afterlife in a man-sized beer bottle because you were known for being a drunk. Which also happened.

Nature's Death Trap

Poisonous snakes abound in Ghana. Species such as the cobra and puff adder are native to Ghana, as are pythons, which don't bite but can squeeze their victims to death. So feel free to mosey around in open–toed sandals if you'd like to take a shortcut to your own fantasy coffin. Which will likely be a fat, happy snake.

The reason for customizing coffins that look like rejects of an elaborately bizarre merry-go-round has to do with the Ga's attitudes toward the afterlife. They believe that after death you continue doing the same thing you did in life, and that dearly departed ancestors are powerful entities, so families do all they can to curry favor with soon-to-be influential familial spirits. They also reflect social status and are only visible to the public on the day of a burial (unless you take a peek at a specialty carpenter's workshop filled with huge chickens, cell phones, machine guns, and crabs on the sly). As it may be hard to understand how much of a compliment it is to be stuffed inside a lizard or a soda bottle for eternity, it certainly beats being planted in the dirt inside something that symbolizes our faults. Like, say, a dirty couch covered with empty ice cream containers.

Another popular option is to be buried in *okadi adekai*, or "proverbial coffins," which evoke the traditional maxims of the Ga. Formerly the sole concern of chiefs and priests, it was in 1950 that customized, made-to-order caskets became a thing and made minor celebrities out of the artisans who created them. Coffin makers such as Kudjoe Affutu, Daniel Mensah, and Paa Joe have been featured in Western documentaries, appeared at various international events, and have had their handiwork displayed in art museums and exhibitions world-wide. Paa Joe (real name Joseph Ashong) has been in the fantasy coffin–making business since 1974, after learning the trade from his uncle. Former UN secretary-general Kofi Annan and ex-US presidents Bill Clinton and Jimmy Carter are fans of his work. Carter even purchased two coffins for himself, presumably in the shape of a peanut. If you'd like to see Joe's creations in person, he continues to tour globally with his son and an apprentice and includes American campuses on his itinerary.

The concept of whimsical coffins is certainly a viable option for those who want to go out with a little bit of panache. In recent years it's spread beyond the confines of West Africa. So if you're looking to spice up your funeral by being buried in a seven-foot Xbox controller or a gargantuan seven-layer burrito, you don't have to travel all the way to Ghana. Inspired by the creativity of the Ga, novelty corpse receptacles are gaining in popularity. Companies such as Crazy Coffins in the United

Three Other Places Where Funerals Are a Festive Affair

- Mexico's brightly colored, flowery graveyards to welcome the dead.
- Botswana drinking binge following a funeral, affectionately called the "after–tears drinking spree."
- Bali's flaming bulls, where the body of the deceased returns to the earth and its soul sparks up.

Kingdom offer the chance to become one with the worms in anything from a dilapidated Yugo to a heavy metal guitar to a replica of the Starship *Enterprise* from Star Trek. Or you could just buy a KISS Kasket from rock star Gene Simmons, if you're not too picky about your reception at whatever final destination you believe you'll be arriving at.

FINGER CUTTING

Expressing Anguish via Amputation

PAPUA NEW GUINEA According to the Kübler-Ross psychological model, the five stages of grief are denial, anger, bargaining, depression, and acceptance. And in Papua New Guinea, there's a sixth: lopping off the tip of your finger at the joint. The Dani tribe, like some other cultures, believes that causing yourself physical pain is an important way of expressing emotional pain. The particular way they choose to inflict it is by tying a string around the upper half of an unlucky digit for about thirty minutes until it goes numb. At least numb enough to cut down on the screaming when the axe comes down and the open flesh gets cauterized in fire.

The finger-cutting custom is specific to women in Dani society, who sacrifice their bones and flesh after the death of a child or other member of the family. The practice is also believed to be helpful in both pleasing and driving away any unwanted spirits of the afterlife, presumably should the family member in question be a mother-in-law. All right, so it's not helpful in pursuing a career that requires finger dexterity (which may explain why you see so few Papua New Guineans playing second cello for the New York Philharmonic). But what are a few finger joints among family?

The women don't chop off their own fingers like a desperate survivor of a minor zombie bite in a postapocalyptic

TV series. That task is given to an immediate family member (presumably the one with the best aim and steadiest hand). While there's usually a lot to be said for maintaining one's cultural traditions, it's hard to recommend gory self-mutilation. So it's probably good that this practice is gradually disappearing. After all, what if you were a woman with a large family and something in the area of fifteen relatives died in a matter of a few years? Two handfuls of useless nubs are hard to argue for, and based on many photos of the Dani, that outcome isn't unrealistic.

However, there's another way the folks of Papua New Guinea treat human appendages, one we'd definitely like to see survive into the centuries to come. This one involves the men and their *koteka* (also known as the *horim*, or "penis gourd"). This is an elongated sheath used to simultaneously cover male genitals and make them look more spectacular (imagine the Super Bowl shows!). Tribes can be distinguished by the different ways they wear their *kotekas*, whether they point up, to the side, how girthy they are, and so on. In addition to being

Warring and Dancing in the Cyclops

The Dani reside in the Baliem Valley in the Cyclops Mountains, an area governed by Indonesia like the rest of the island. It's an area that is accessible only by airplane; foreign hikers are increasingly in the area and communing with a culture that's only been in contact with the West since 1938. As remote as their situation is, the valley in which the Dani live is also home to the Art of War and Dance Festival, an event all Papuan tribes attend. These days there's hopefully more dance than there is war, and it's been described by some of the few outsiders to make their way there as "an unforgettable, once-in-a-lifetime experience."

decorative, some of them also serve a practical purpose: You can use them as a place to store money and tobacco. As a bonus, this also seems an excellent way to avoid *sharing* your money and tobacco.

Another ancient and painful tradition of the Papuans is the coming-of-age ritual of bloodletting. When boys in the Sambia tribe reach puberty, it's believed they must be "defeminized" by removing the blood of their mothers. The blood draining, designed to make the boys into masculine warriors, is accomplished in several ways that include shoving sharp reeds up their noses and hollowed-out canes into their necks. It's highly unlikely that these measures prevent any of the boys from becoming gay, unless you factor in the deaths from sudden blood loss.

You might suppose that with customs like the one above that the gay and transgender community of Papua New Guinea is practically nonexistent. Homosexuality is in fact illegal there

Operation Penis Sheath

In the early 1970s, the Indonesian government initiated Operation Koteka, an attempt to make the male natives of Papua New Guinea stop wearing penis gourds and other traditional garb and instead put on T-shirts and shorts like the tourists who showed up to gawk (and who spent a lot of money buying their own *kotekas* to bring home, incidentally). However, the new clothes wound up causing skin diseases because the Papuans had no idea how to wash them. Unsurprisingly, *kotekas* to this day remain prevalent throughout the island.

(punishable by up to fourteen years in prison), but prosecution of gays is becoming increasingly rare. Also, there's an entire village now where those in the LGBT community can finally feel safe. Hanuabada, in the area of the national capital of Port Moresby, is possibly the only place in the country where they can walk the streets openly and feel safe from being assaulted. Only about thirty Gelegele, as they call themselves, live in the village at any one time, but the population fluctuates as others stay temporarily then leave, and there's reason to believe it will increase as attitudes within Papua New Guinea shift.

Also helping to change hearts and minds is a documentary called *Guavas and Bananas: Living Gay in PNG* that's part of the touring PNG Human Rights Film Festival. The filmmaker behind it, Vlad Sokhin, explained how his movie could improve things: "So I think we should talk about these things, we should talk more openly. I know this is still a taboo in Papua New Guinean society but the more we talk about it, it would change things I think."

HANGING COFFINS
It's Safe from Floods At Least

PHILIPPINES Just about every culture throughout history, no matter what peculiar and disturbing preparations went into getting the bodies ready beforehand, has made it a priority to put their dead into the ground. It just makes sense, as it deals with multiple issues like disease, odor, and the possibility of an undignified public dismemberment by animals. Not everyone has traditionally buried their dear departed in the cold earth, however. For instance, the people of the Igorot tribe in the northern Philippines, while still placing the corpses of their loved ones into coffins, prefer to tie them to the sides of cliffs to stay for as long as the weather allows. Or at least until the termites find a way to get up there.

The hanging coffins, which can be found in Echo Valley in the municipality of Sagada, can be so high up they're barely visible to the naked eye, or low enough to give tourists an alarming eyeful. It's believed that the Igorots have been doing this for over two thousand years, well before the arrival of the Spanish, and they're still putting boxes up on cliffs to this day. As for why, the whole "the higher up you go, the closer you are to heaven" aspect is only part of the answer. Another reason for keeping them above ground had to do with the wet climate.

The moist soil isn't conducive to burial. And enemies might want to steal their heads as trophies. Yeah, that one's probably the most understandable out of the bunch.

Adding to the atmosphere in the foreboding Echo Valley gorge is a profound lack of sunlight. And of course there's a very real risk that one of the coffins may come crashing down and spill its contents in the middle of your macabre sightseeing tour. The coffins aren't meant to last up in the clouds forever. Since the families tie the wooden containers with vines, they know the coffins'll eventually return to terra firma. You know, to make space for new generations of the dangling dead.

The coffins themselves are small. It's not because they contain children or that the people inside are stunted in some way. The bodies are folded up and inserted in the fetal position, in the belief that everyone should exit this plane the same way they entered it. It's also the job of the person who'll one day be going inside to do some carving on his own coffin. If he procrastinates too much a relative will take over the task. Hopefully not a teenager, who might carve flames and dragons and make the whole thing look like an airbrushed panel van from the 1970s.

Further Proving You Can't Take It with You

They hang up coffins in central China too. The *xuanguan* (coffins) of the eastern province of Fujian and other areas are wedged into crevasses, propped up by pounded-in cantilevered stakes, or piled up on stacks way up high in a cave. People have been doing it for about three thousand years, but we still don't know how they got the things up there.

The Fashionable Dead

On the island of Mindoro, the Hanunuo Mangyan tribe place the dead on display. In the practice of *kutkot*, family members dig up the bodies of their expired relatives every year and dress them in new clothes. They then arrange the remains into a *sinakot*, which is their best attempt at making them look like a living human instead of a desiccated cadaver. While the tradition still has its adherents, they are decreasing by the year. Nonetheless, travelers should be wary of asking brightly clothed elderly strangers how they manage to stay so slim.

When the time comes to bring the recently deceased to the place where their coffin is to hang, a procession of family and friends have to fend off mourners trying to claw at the corpse. It's not that they're overcome by grief; rather they're trying to get the blood of the expired party on their hands to smear on themselves. It's thought that this will transfer the dead person's skills to the living. You'd think one of those skills that gets passed on would be increased politeness at funeral processions.

A final curious thing one may notice at Igorot cemeteries (in case you didn't think a cliff filled with suspended corpses was enough) is the wooden chairs that are tied up there alongside the coffins. They're called "death chairs" (obviously), and the bodies are put on them before getting crammed into the tiny coffins. Immediately after death, the cadavers are seated in these *sangadils*, secured, and covered in a blanket. After getting properly propped and ready for viewing, the occupant of the chair is faced toward the front door so visiting relatives and friends can pay their respects. This procedure can last a few days, which can present some complications when things get a little too...odiferous. So to prevent rapid decomposition and unpleasant smells, the body is smoked like a Black Forest ham. While the Igorots were most certainly headhunters in the distant past, cannibalism is not believed to have been part of their lifestyle. Not to say the actual cannibals in the area weren't jealous of their barbecuing skills.

MUMMIFICATION

Way More Hardcore Than the Paleo Diet

JAPAN

While Egypt's mummies get all the press, we shouldn't forget that they're not the only folks into preserving their dead bodies for posterity. Transforming one's relatives into creepy relics for future generations of archaeologists to yank out of their tombs and put on display for museum patrons to leer at has been a time-honored tradition in multiple cultures over the course of millennia. Self-mummification, however, is quite a bit rarer. Mostly because it's one thing to be given the treatment by corpse-pickling experts after you've already breathed your last breath, but quite another to do the job yourself while you're still very much alive.

Sokushinbutsu is the Japanese word that refers to the attempts in the past by Buddhist monks to turn themselves into mummies. Specifically, the monks ate only certain foods that preserved the body. The monks who took these measures were also called "tree eaters," due to the fact that such a diet included things like bark, pine needles, and resin. Yum! Additionally, they ate herbs and nuts that contained toxins in order to counter bacterial growth; along with tea made from the same sap used to make lacquer, which would basically perform the same function as embalming fluid. It must have been

Shine On, You Crazy Urn

Currently, Japan has the highest cremation rate in the world. But not everyone is satisfied with just tossing Grandma and Grandpa up on the mantel to
gather dust. Thus, the Japanese have incorporated their love of high technology into the equation and created electronic cemeteries, which resemble a
laser light show at the planetarium more than a place of solemn reflection.
Take the Ruriden columbarium in Tokyo, for example, which houses around two
thousand small altars that not only contain a deceased person's ashes; they
also light up whenever a relative enters the building with a smart card. We're
sure someone has already thought of rigging the system so that the altars all
light up to the rhythm of Pink Floyd music, but we have to go on the record
and affirm that this would probably be in poor taste.

hard to do this. However, if part of their belief system included
something like "the mortician industry is nothing more than a
greedy racket," then the effort was certainly worth it in the
long run.

It's believed that hundreds of monks over the course of
hundreds of years have tried the self-mummification process,
but only twenty-four favorable outcomes have ever been
recorded—not exactly a staggering success rate. In some of
those cases the preservation may have had more to do with a
cold, arid climate than the type of tree-based diet that would
make the most dedicated vegan gag. Practitioners did not consider the process suicide but rather a path toward enlighten-
ment (which is a little sad, considering only a tiny percentage
pulled it off). The failure rate becomes especially depressing

when you learn about the time commitment involved. For many of the monks it would take years of nibbling forest detritus and near-inedible carpentry flotsam before they died of malnutrition and poison. But it's said the pain and the hunger pangs were just part of the whole ordeal of "passing into the state of nirvana."

It's unlikely that one would find a Buddhist monk suffering through *sokushinbutsu* today, although that's not to say Japan doesn't still have its fair share of people obsessed with their path to the hereafter. The term *shukatsu*, a play on the Japanese word for "job hunting," refers to meticulously planning your own funeral arrangements. With an aging population and declining birth rate, such concerns are understandable and definitely profitable for those in the funeral business. There

Do AIBOs Dream Electric Dreams?

If you have ever sat around wondering just how much the Japanese love robots, consider this. AIBO, the world's first home entertainment robot dog with a "personality," first appeared in 1999 and was a very popular product but has since stopped being produced. That means there are a lot of "dead" AIBOs out there, and many of them have been sent back to the company responsible for their manufacture, A-Fun. Instead of tossing all the techno pooches onto a landfill or lighting them on fire in a dumpster, A-Fun sent them to a Buddhist temple to receive a traditional funeral. A priest at the location commented on the situation, stating, "All things have a bit of soul." If you think it was a little strange for a profit-motivated company to express this sort of sentimentality over a collection of plastic and wires, be comforted in the fact that after the service the AIBOs were cannibalized for parts to be used in other contraptions and possibly for the American relaunch of a new generation of toy robot dogs.

are even conventions and expos where attendees can test out coffins, try on outfits they'd like to be buried in, and get a makeover to see how they'd look at an open-casket viewing. Now if someone could take this concept to suburban malls and charge goth kids admission, there might just be a fortune to be made.

If you ever find yourself attending a Japanese funeral, whether it be for a guy who ossified himself via a crappy diet of lumberyard sweepings or one for cybernetic canines, there are several important rules of etiquette to be aware of. Wearing black is standard, as it is in Western funerals. What's not in line with what you're used to is the gift giving. It's customary to hand over an envelope containing cash to the family. Make sure the number of notes as well as the total amount are in odd-numbered amounts (and somewhere between 5,000–30,000 yen) for luck. Avoid anything that might add up to the number four; as mentioned in another entry, it's the opposite of lucky despite how appropriate it may seem for the occasion). If you're feeling a little ripped off, be sure to stick around for the entirety of the wake, as guests are given a gift upon departure, which is usually around a quarter to half the worth of the money you put in the envelope earlier. So it's not that bad a deal overall and definitely a better payoff than spending years of your life trying to eat yourself into shriveled immortality and ending up worm food like everyone else.

DEATH BEADS

Not Just for Curtains Anymore

If you've been wondering what kind of jewelry to wear, we've got a suggestion: Melt your departed loved ones down into beads and string them around your neck or wrist.

Like Japan, South Korea has an aging population with too few babies being born to close the gap. In fact, it's accumulating senior citizens faster than any other developed country, since a low birth rate is one of their most alarming statistics. While Japan's population is confined to a series of islands, South Korea is also constrained by geographical limits—in its case a peninsula (and a madcap, murderous dictatorship to the north). So graveyards have given way to more creative ways of honoring the departed. The current trend is melting Grandpa down into something called a death bead.

The death bead is the brainchild of a company called Bonhyang. They present an alternative to the traditional practice of keeping the ashes of the dead in urns. Instead, the remains are heated up and molded into glass bits that "have the look of beluga caviar," according to Jung-yoon Choi of the *Los Angeles Times*. The process itself costs just a bit under $1,000. The beads resemble edible fish eggs and come in festive hues such as blue, green, pink, and black. If the one you received changes color according to your mood, you may consider contacting an exorcist.

The idea behind death beads is not to string fallen relatives onto a friendship bracelet for wagering and trading among your pals but to create a more decorative and less depressing way of keeping your late ancestors close at hand. According to the CEO of the company, Bae Jae-yul, "You don't feel that these beads are creepy or scary. In fact, there's a holiness and warmth to them." If you feel actual warmth, however, we would again recommend seeking the assistance of trained clergy. So far it appears the product is a big hit in a country where only three out of ten corpses are put in the ground. Also helping Bonhyang's bottom line is the law enacted in 2000, mandating that anyone buried after that year must be dug up sixty years after the fact. On a side note, you might want to postpone your 2060 South Korean vacation until 2061, as things are going to be a little weird over there for the twelve months prior.

⦿ The Eternal Worker's Paradise

The Democratic People's Republic of Korea (the alternate way to say Kim Jong-un's North Korean House of Horrors) has its own distinct method of sending their faithful citizens to Communist Heaven. According to a defector, the first step is to stuff the ears and nose with cotton to prevent unsightly leakage. Then the mouth is filled with rice for a snack on the way to the Marxist promised land. The body is then laid on top of a coffin for three days while family members sit nearby, watching in case the body returns to life (which seems fairly unlikely after the first couple steps, but it is eminently possible considering the state of North Korean medical science). If day three rolls around with nary a wiggle, it's finally time for a burial or cremation.

🔍 Cry or Else, Citizen

When Kim Jong-Il (North Korea's second supreme leader after his father, Kim Il-sung) passed away in 2011, there was so much public grief on display one would have thought the state media was pumping an overdubbed version of *Old Yeller* onto every television set in the nation. Was all the wailing and histrionic pavement-pounding for real, some form of mass hysteria, or a fervent desire to avoid being sent to a gulag for failure to be sufficiently emotional? Possibly all of the above. But whatever one's true opinion of the regime, it definitely would have been one of the worst times in recorded history to suddenly remember a funny story someone told at work the day before.

Bae had his own parents dug up to be transformed into death beads, demonstrating both a sincere belief in his product and an impressive knack for self-promotion. While attempts to sell the idea of superheating your kin into postmortem marbles have been made in the United States, Europe, and Japan, the concept hasn't caught on as much as in Bae's homeland. Critics feel that the whole thing is just too synthetic and that the very notion prevents the dead from returning to their natural state. However, whether sales numbers may be boosted by printing Hello Kitty logos or smiley faces on the beads probably has yet to be tested. Bae believes his beads will have an advantage against any upstart competition because his rivals "add minerals" (instead of, you know, um...love?).

Being close to a loved one forever in bead form may resonate among the South Koreans in part because of a more traditional belief, one that requires that family members must also be in proximity to the dying immediately prior to their passing. If they're not present during this time the deceased risks turning into a wandering spirit called a *kaekkvi*. However, as far as spooks go, this isn't too bad. It's certainly a better fate than winding up as one of neighboring China's more unsavory denizens of the supernatural realm. Such as the *chòuk u gu* (a "foul-mouthed" spirit with breath that disgusts even itself) or the *y ng gu* (a "tumor ghost," which must feed on the pus from its own malignant growths).

Oh, and there's plenty more involved where an old-school South Korean funeral is concerned. When the actual death does occur, copious and exaggerated weeping, called *kok*, is required as the deceased's clothing is removed, taken to the roof, and pointed north while their name is chanted three times. The body, in turn, is pointed so the head is facing south. After a cleaning ritual called *seup*, which includes hair and nail clippings being stored in a bag, the body is dressed for burial with rice, beads, and three coins, which are placed in the mouth. There is a lot we're glossing over here, with many other rites to be observed. So if you'd prefer a simpler farewell you might consider just jumping into an active volcano or something.

MORTUARY TOTEM POLES

I Can See My House from Here for Eternity

CANADA

When you think of the native peoples of Alaska and British Columbia, one of the first things that comes to mind along with icy igloos and delicious *mukluk* is the majestic totem pole. As an imposing tower of symbolic art, the stylized North American animals and mythical creatures carved from wood stir the imagination while giving bold representation to the heritage and family lineages of the craftspeople who erected them. Think of them as huge, vertical coats of arms. Oh, and sometimes they totally stuffed dead people up there at the tippy top.

The Haida people (of the Haida Gwaii Archipelago off the coast of British Columbia) are remembered as some of the finest practitioners of the art of totem pole construction. They are also remembered for thinking outside the box in terms of what a totem pole could be. By building special versions to be "mortuary poles," they stored the remains of their dead in them. Which there were a lot of, by the way, after smallpox decimated their population in 1862 and left many villages empty of most everything but the poles. They might have been left there to rot, but in the 1950s efforts were made by concerned academics to save the remaining Haida structures from decay. Thus many of the delicate artworks were transported to the

University of British Columbia...to continue decomposing in sheds after being heavily damaged in transport.

Far and away the rarest form of totem poles, mortuary poles are also generally higher than any of the six other types. These are:

- House frontal poles
- House posts
- Memorial poles
- Welcome poles
- A kind of "screw you, buddy" pole we'll talk about soon

They can reach up to seventy feet in length, and in addition to serving as a final resting place (barring high winds) for a person of honor, they also signify who the next of kin is. Either ashes or an entire body may be stored in a box at the very top.

The Pole of Shame

Probably the most entertaining form of totem pole, unless you get a big kick out of looking for corpses way up high on a stick, are those designed to mercilessly mock somebody. Ridicule or shame poles are erected to publicly embarrass an individual, usually because that person failed to pay a debt. Jeering at entire groups is not unheard of, however. Or giant corporations. Case in point: In 2007, a shame pole was put up for the anniversary of the catastrophic *Exxon Valdez* oil spill. At the top was an upside–down carving of the former Exxon CEO, Lee Raymond, with an elongated nose in the style of a certain famous lying puppet.

Happy Birthday! Now March

Forcing old folks to shuffle onto ice floes to die at sea isn't some legend—it's a practice called senicide and did in fact occur among the Inuit and Yuit tribes of Greenland/Alaska. While other tribes found the custom to be as abhorrent as you hopefully do, when resources were scarce, the elderly who could no longer contribute were sometimes eliminated by their own hand or another's. While literally marching them onto ice floes might be a slight exaggeration (a belief made popular via old movies), the end result was the same. Although for many this was probably a much better fate than spending the remainder of their years in Florida.

We have to assume there's some sort of device up there to ward off eagles in the same way that bird feeders have those little plastic guards to keep squirrels at bay.

Because we all know you want to know more about those shame poles, here's another fun story about them. Remember Secretary of State William H. Seward? The guy who purchased Alaska? Which commentators referred to as "Seward's Folly"? Yeah, him. Well, the guy who bought the entire state of Alaska from the Russians for just seven million bucks wasn't looked upon too kindly by his Tlingit tribal hosts after he was deemed insufficiently grateful and reciprocal when they threw a potlatch ceremonial feast in his honor. So, naturally, they immortalized him in a shame pole, where his sad-looking figure sits on top with a red nose and ears to symbolize his penchant for being a penny-pinching jerk.

Not just anyone got the pole treatment, mind you. Only the highest-ranking members of Haida society got that privilege. A harsh environment can lead to harsh customs, it seems, as regular folks were generally tossed into mass graves, while their slaves were chucked into the Pacific as orca chow. However, although some tribes in the region were labeled as savage cannibals back in the 1800s, those reports were overblown and a libelous excuse for their subjugation. During that time the majority of people eating other people were British explorers. Such as in the tragic case of Sir John Franklin's expedition, which took place in 1845. Setting out in the suitably named ships HMS *Erebus* and HMS *Terror*, the crews became icebound and eventually succumbed to the elements. But not before dining on each other to the point where bones were broken to extract the marrow. It almost makes getting prodded out onto a sheet of ice to fend off polar bears seem like a pleasant way to go.

DRIVE-THROUGH FUNERALS

Would You Like Flowers with That?

UNITED STATES Want breakfast, lunch, or dinner? Go to a drive-through. Got business at the bank? Go to a drive-through. Prescription needs filling? Go to a drive-through. You can also pick up your liquor out of a window in some states, and there's even the Tunnel of Love drive-through nuptials at A Little White Wedding Chapel in Las Vegas. You might wonder what other industry could possibly take advantage of this modern marvel of motorized ministration. If you said "funerals," and then smiled at the joke, we regret to inform you that such a thing does in fact exist and it is not a giggling matter. There are drive-through funerals.

While the Vegas wedding setup is obviously a tongue-in-cheek operation, Adams Funeral Home in Compton, California, was serious—dead serious—when they expanded their business to accommodate those wanting a more streamlined experience when offering their respects to the dearly departed. If you're up to speed on your old-school gangsta rap, you may recognize Compton as a locale where...well, let's just say it's not going to land on the list of safest cities anytime soon. As a result, it can sometimes be hazardous for family members of crime victims to mourn in a group right out in the open. Now there's an option to roll through the funeral service

Fast-Food Felonies

For those needing to interact through a window with something even more repugnant than a corpse, Kocian Law Group of Manchester, Connecticut, lets you consult with an attorney in the same efficient manner. Occupying what was once the site of a Kenny Rogers Roasters chicken restaurant, the new residents decided to keep the drive—through window in place to accommodate injured clients who might find it easier to stay inside their vehicles (which may or may not be an ambulance, thereby eliminating the need for chasing). Their services are also available on nights and weekends, presumably in case you'd like to file one of the lawsuits on their value menu.

in a vehicle. Providing another safety feature for their clientele, the glass partitions through which visitors may view the deceased are bulletproof.

An area landmark since the mid-seventies, Adams Funeral Home was founded by the late Robert Lee Adams Sr. and is now operated by his widow, Peggy. She described the services her business offers to the *Los Angeles Times* in 2011: "It's a unique feature that sets us aside from other funeral parlors. You can come by after work, you don't need to deal with parking, you can sign the book outside, and the family knows that you paid your respects. It's a convenience thing." This convenience extends to the disabled, as funeral attendees have been known to ride their wheelchairs through as part of the motorized procession.

Although there may be a few other drive-through funeral parlors in existence, scattered throughout the United States and elsewhere, Robert Lee Adams Sr. can be credited with coming up with the novel idea. A bust of his noble countenance greets visitors near the entrance, much like he must have done in person when he was a Southern California politician.

Perhaps you are considering giving a loved one over to Adams's expert care so that friends and family might pay their respects without having to bother to open the doors on their minivans. If so, be aware that the limited height and width of the viewing lane cannot accommodate larger vehicles like tour buses, Winnebagos, or tractor trailers. Any long-haul truckers in your family should probably rent a sensible hatchback or moped for the occasion. Just advise motorcyclists that it's more respectful if they remove their helmet (or at least lift the visor) before passing through.

The Windy City of Chicago got its very own drive-through memorial option in 1989, when Gatling's Chapel gave mourners on the city's South Side the option to grieve on the go.

Big in Japan

The drive-through funeral concept seems to have also caught on in Japan. It's unknown if they took their inspiration from the Compton originators, but the overall experience is about the same. Although the Kankon Sousai Aichi Group in Nagano is a little more high-tech, with touch screen sign-ins and electronic incense burners. The handicapped access is again a major selling point (although the drive-by shooting avoidance aspect doesn't really enter into the equation). In terms of efficiency, the head of the company, Masao Ogiwara, makes a bold claim: "All in all, it will cut down the time it takes to attend a funeral by around one-fourth or one-fifth." And surely with a little ingenuity and perseverance, the prospect of a full one-third reduction may one day appear on the horizon.

The owner, Lafayette Gatling, described his motivations to *The New York Times*: "The working person doesn't have time to come in. They want to see the body, but they don't want to have to wait. I always thought there should be some way they could see the body any time they want." We can only assume he's speaking in the pre-burial sense.

The notion of saying your final farewells to your embalmed loved ones without having to leave the comfort of a luxury sedan does seem to make a lot of sense when you consider Chicago's remorseless wintertime temperatures. Michigan's weather also explains why they got their own version in Saginaw in 2014. The cold doesn't do much to explain why the town of New Roads in muggy Louisiana needed one, however. The owner of the Verrett's-Pointe Coupee Funeral Home claims they are merely filling the market niche for "people who didn't have time to dress." Or perhaps the alligator population, combined with encroachment from the invasive pythons of Florida, are making this the only option that keeps their customers' open-casket viewings safe from a public devouring.

INDEX

Index

ABOUT THE AUTHOR

E. Reid Ross is an editor/columnist at Cracked.com. His other books include *Nature Is the Worst: 500 Reasons You'll Never Want to Go Outside Again*. He has a background in military intelligence and law enforcement, and currently resides in Maryland with a family that includes a combination of hominids, canines, felines, and marsupials.